OVERTHINKING DISORDER

Increase Your Self-motivation, Silence Your Inner Criticism

(Learn How to Control Your Emotions Throughout with Brainwash Techniques)

Eric Walker

I0095592

Published by Knowledge Icons

Eric Walker

Overthinking Disorder: Increase Your Self-motivation, Silence Your Inner Criticism (Learn How to Control Your Emotions Throughout with Brainwash Techniques)

ISBN 978-1-990084-70-6

Legal & Disclaimer

The information contained in this book is not designed to replace or take the place of any form of medicine or professional medical advice. The information in this book has been provided for educational and entertainment purposes only.

The information contained in this book has been compiled from sources deemed reliable, and it is accurate to the best of the Author's knowledge; however, the Author cannot guarantee its accuracy and validity and cannot be held liable for any errors or omissions. Changes are periodically made to this book. You must consult your doctor or get professional medical advice before using any of the

TABLE OF CONTENTS

INTRODUCTION 1

CHAPTER 1: WHAT IS OVERTHINKING? 4

CHAPTER 2: POSITIVE THINKING VS. POSITIVE SPEAKING 32

CHAPTER 3: IDENTIFY YOUR WORRIES AND DEAL WITH

THEM 37

CHAPTER 4: THE FUTILITY AND FATALITY OF WORRY 44

CHAPTER 5: WHAT ARE THE SYMPTOMS OF

OVERTHINKING? 59

CHAPTER 6: ANXIETY 63

CHAPTER 7: TAKING CONTROL OF YOUR THOUGHTS 77

CHAPTER 8: OVER THINKING ARE YOU ALWAYS IN YOUR

OWN HEAD 102

CHAPTER 9: HOW YOUR MIND WORKS AND WHY YOU

THINK THE WAY YOU DO 120

CHAPTER 10: WHAT IN THE WORLD IS GOING ON? 130

CHAPTER 11: NEGATIVE EMOTIONS 141

CHAPTER 12: WHAT IS OVERTHINKING AND WHAT ARE

THE CAUSES? 146

CHAPTER 13: WHAT IS OVERTHINKING?........................ 159

CHAPTER 14: HOW TO DE-CLUTTER YOUR MIND........... 165

CHAPTER 15: FOODS FOR THE BRAIN 173

CONCLUSION.. 201

Introduction

As the name implies, overthinking simply means thinking too much. In reality, when you spend more time thinking instead of acting and engaging in other activities, then you're overthinking. You can find yourself analyzing, commenting, and repeating the same thoughts over and over again, rather than taking action, then you're overthinking. Such bad habits can hinder your progress, leaving one unproductive.

Each individual will experience overthinking differently and no two people overthink the same way. But generally, all those who overthink will agree that the quality of their life has been affected by their inability to control their negative thoughts and emotions. Such habits make it very difficult for the majority of the individuals to socialize, be productive at work, or enjoy hobbies due to the enormous amount of time and energy their mind consumes on a specific line of thoughts. Such uncontrolled emotions can be very harmful to the individual's mental health.

Overthinking makes it more difficult to make new friends and to keep friends; you will find it difficult to converse with them because you're overly concerned about what to say or what to do to keep the conversation going. Some individuals who are affected by this disorder may find it challenging to participate in general conversations or to interact with others even in a normal environment. In addition, some may have trouble keeping an appointment or going to the store. This kind of thinking wastes time and drains your energy, thereby preventing you from taking action or exploring new ideas. It also hinders progress in life. This can be compared to attaching a chain that is connected to a pole around your waist and then running in circles you will be busy but not productive. Overthinking will disable your capacity to make sound decisions.

Under such circumstances, you're more likely to be worried, anxious, and devoid of inner peace of mind. However, when you stop overthinking, you will become more productive, happy, and will enjoy more peace.

Chapter 1: What Is Overthinking?

~ Anxiety is the dizziness of freedom. ~
- Soren Kierkegaard, the Concept of Anxiety: A Simple Psychologically Orienting Deliberation on the Dogmatic Issue of Hereditary Sin

Is overthinking a disorder or an anxiety disorder?

The easy answer is no, overthinking is not a mental disorder. Overthinking is a term that means a person spends too long thinking and worrying about certain issues or situations. He or she gets stuck thinking about a problem or situation instead of putting that time and energy into a resolution or moving on. This can lead to a feeling of anxiety and depression if not addressed.

Overthinking can be a symptom of some anxiety disorders, but it can also be a sign of simply being overwhelmed. Sometimes a nudge or taking an alternate path is needed to get moving again. But it's really difficult to nudge your own self out of a slump or find an alternate path never traveled. That is where this book can help you. We are going to review different exercises and techniques for recognizing and dealing with emotional stress.

Everyone, at different times in their lives, has felt anxious or nervous about facing stressful situations. Taking final exams, speaking in front of a crowd, meeting new people, and dating are examples of a few stress-inducing activities. People can also overthink situations like major purchases (car, home, or boat), changing careers, new relationship, or how children should spend the summer. That does not necessarily lead to chronic overthinking or any anxiety disorder. It's normal to be stressed about some of life's events.

Construction Ahead!

Getting control of overthinking is all about creating safe places for you - both physically and emotionally. Building confidence in your abilities to express emotions, learn to handle differences before they build into confrontational situations, and feel free to set new exciting goals for your life.

This is not going to happen overnight. For one thing, you have to learn why you overthink certain problems and/or situations. Then, you must learn how to break the habits that feed the overthinking. It is said that it takes seventeen days to break a habit. But those of us who have had to quit smoking or drinking, or some other destructive habit know it is something we deal with on a daily bases.

Does that thought of dealing with something on a daily bases upset up? Does it drain your energy or stop you dead in your tracks from trying to change a habit?

Turn those thoughts around. Do it right now. You are going to learn to use each day to improve your coping skills to keep you on track to attain your goals. That is exciting! Each day you have a chance to add on to your life and enhance it in any direction you choose.

This is a process you can share with the entire family after you have mastered the skills. When you are having a conflict with a child, spouse, or other loved one, you will be able to decide just how you want to resolve the situation. Rather than the same old routine of bickering or procrastinating you will be able to take decisive action and for the most part avoid anxiety-producing stress.

Think of this as a user's manual for daily maintenance. Follow the directions, put in the work to complete the exercises, and your life will run smoother. Who doesn't want that? Every day you are constructing a better version of yourself.

Blue Prints for Life

If someone plunked a computer down in front of you and said: "Fix this please, it stopped working." Unless you're a hardware technician you probably wouldn't know where to start without some sort of Care and Maintenance manual. Well, the same goes for overthinking. Most folks think they are being helpful, giving you practical advice when they say something like "just stop thinking about it", or "think about something else, instead" or "just let it go." As if it's that easy. Click, flip the thought switch to off and move on.

Would that it was that simple. Eventually, you do have to "let it go", but first you must learn how to do that with success and confidence. For some, reading this book and doing the exercises will be enough to help break old, harmful habits, and build new, life-enhancing habits.

For others, you may find that these exercises lead you to realize that some professional counseling is a better option. When you discuss the health portion of the action plan with your physician, he might suggest treatment that will help you achieve your goals even faster.

~ Don't worry if people think you're crazy. You are crazy. You have that kind of intoxicating insanity that lets other people dream outside of the lines and become who they're destined to be. ~

- Jennifer Elisabeth, Born Ready: Unleash Your Inner Dream Girl

Before we move on with our explanation of overthinking let's look briefly at anxiety disorders and make a clear distinction between the two.

Some common anxiety disorders include:

Panic disorder: This may also be referred to as a panic attack or an anxiety attack. A panic attack can sometimes feel like a heart attack due to similar symptoms. You may feel a rapid or irregular heartbeat, accompanied by sweating and chest pains. If you ever experience this call 911 emergency. You can't really tell the difference between a panic attack and an actual heart attack.

Social anxiety disorder: Also referred to as a social phobia. You may feel worried and self-conscious about daily social situations such as after-work gatherings, club meetings, holiday parties, social gatherings with work colleagues, or friends and family. The feeling that others are judging you or an overwhelming fear of being embarrassed or ridiculed at social gatherings is also a sign of this disorder.

Generalized anxiety disorder: Excessive tension and worry with little or no reason. A constant feeling of doom when you know that there are no current events that should cause this feeling.

Specific phobias: Fear of animals, heights, small closed-in places, or certain objects or situations. These fears can become so overwhelming that you start to avoid activities in your life.

If you or someone you love find any of the above disorders affecting your daily life. If the anxiety is preventing you from having close friends, dating, participating in hobbies, isolating you from everyday life events, please seek counseling. Don't let something that is easily corrected steal another day of your life. We will speak more about counseling later in this chapter.

Overthinking & Relationships

There are specific signs that can alert you to the fact that you or someone you love overthink issues and situations. Before we review the list of behavior that can signal to overthink, let's look at an example of other behaviors that can snare an over-thinker.

Think about recent conversations you have had with friends or family. Do you tend to somehow always work the conversation around to the same several topics? Perhaps you discuss them at length but never seem to find a solution? Or, you may find yourself discussing other friend's issues, wondering why he or she put up with a certain situation. You two are great at solving other people's problems, but not your own. This type of revisiting of the same topics can be a sign of two overthinkers working together. Be on the lookout for the signs of the following types of relationships. The dynamics can add to problems with overthinking.

The Independent Relationship

This type of relationship can be problematic for people who have been single for quite a while and are used to fending for themselves. Women in particular who have battled their way up the corporate ladder or are making a living in what is seen as a male-centric career.

This person is used to getting the job done on time and under budget. No waiting for the door to be open, discussing where to go, or what to do. This is a person who is used to being in charge because it is his or her job.

Unfortunately, that's not what you want to call your strongest quality for friendship or a romantic relationship. This person needs to learn the art of compromise, selflessness, and sacrifice. Yes, independence is good. You want your partner to be able to function when you are not around. But total independence is a sign of rough roads ahead.

Co-Dependency

Quite the opposite of the Independent Relationship is the Co-Dependent Relationship. In this dynamic, the two partners cannot seem to function apart. It's not a matter of having two halves of one skill set where one person complements the other (writer/editor). No, it's more a lack of trust from security and self-confidence issues. Both couples may have some growing up to do but can't because they are attached at the hip.

Open Relationships

I think these have been around for thousands of years (see pre-arranged marriages), but everything that is old is new again. Sometime back in the 1970s the term Open Marriage came to mean a marriage between two people where extra-marital affairs were allowed and even encouraged.

There is still a tremendous about of debate surrounding this concept as to the benefits. But, for the most part, if you and your partner are taking part in this type of relationship one or both of you are probably not ready for a serious commitment.

The Long Distance Relationship

These rarely work without a solid timeline as to when the two partners will reunite.

For example, one partner is sent by their company to implement a project for a period of nine months. This can work if the company is able to fly one or other half of the family for visits. Even then the relationship can be in for some rough times.

If it's a matter of a new job opportunity and one person moves ahead with the other to follow those relationships don't usually fair as well. Typically, one of the partners meets someone else in his or her everyday routine who eventually replaces the original partner. Absence doesn't necessarily make the heart grow fonder.

The Changing Relationship

This relationship is where friends or partners try to change themselves to fit the other's needs. They are constantly adjusting, hobbies, exercise routines, looks, routines, and interest in order to please the other partner. If you have to change your personality to have someone like you, it's not a real friendship or partnership.

Instead of the adult path of compromise, acceptance, and sacrifice, they would rather keep shifting to please one another. One or both of the participants in this relationship need to look at his or her fear of confrontation in the eye and work through it until they feel comfortable being themselves.

If left to continue on to its inevitable outcome the friend or partner bending themselves out of shape will eventually return to their natural self. When this happens, he or she can snap back so hard that they flatten the other partner emotionally. Many times, the other partner had no idea that this person was altering his or herself to please. The change in attitude comes as a complete surprise and the other partner can be left dumbfounded.

Toxic Relationships

There was a case where two friends did a version of what is described above. They enjoyed each other's company and had hobbies in common. After the getting to know each other period - work, family, marriage, divorce, pets, moves, college, etc., their conversations started coming back around to the fact that they had some past trauma in common and how that trauma had affected their lives.

Sharing traumatic situations can be therapeutic and cathartic if you can share, listen, and move on. Move on being the operative word here. But when two over-thinkers get together a situation can develop where they fuel each other's problems rather than help. That is what happened to the two friends. Eventually, they started getting really irritated with each other's inability to move on. Their friendship became toxic, hurtful words were exchanged, and the friendship ended rather abruptly.

These were not two awful people who set out to hurt one another or anybody else for that matter. They both simply had too many unresolved problems of their own to help one another.

Just Friends for Now ...

This is not such a bad place to be as long as both parties realize that's all the relationship is and nothing more. This type of relationship can bring healing to two people who are recovering from bad relationships and are looking for some fun and understanding.

The Dominant/Submissive Relationship

This is exactly what it sounds like one partner controls the other in all things.

Another recipe for disaster when it comes to a serious relationship. This is not to be confused with a game of slap and tickle with bracelets and whips. That is a different subject matter altogether and usually takes place between consenting adults.

In a dominant/submissive relationship, the dominant partner takes away the freedoms of the submissive partner. No choices, no say in household, career, money, or future planning decisions. This can be a soul-crushing situation for the submissive partner and anyone finding themselves in this type of relationship should seek help.

Best Friends Relationship

This is not referring to a platonic relationship which most of us has or had with classmates, co-workers, or relatives.

A Best Friends Relationship is a term for an adult couple who are fine talking and connecting emotionally, but there is a serious lack of intimacy. Healthy sex life is an important part of any couple's relationship and without that component is doomed to fail.

The Sexual Relationship

This relationship is the exact opposite of the Best Friends Relationship. This is a relationship where two people are clearly looking for sex and no other connection. Again, this is great if you can handle it. I've found that one partner usually ends up with the short end of the straw wishing for more of a connection.

The Truly Compatible Relationship

This is the relationship most of us aspire to. A healthy relationship based on trust, love, and understanding. And it takes a tremendous amount of work to maintain. Those words used earlier such as selflessness, sacrifice, compassion, and understanding are the bedrock of this relationship.

We aren't going to discuss the different relationship types of in-depth, but the dynamics of a relationship are an important factor for you to consider while researching overthinking.

~ If you want to conquer the anxiety of life, live in the moment, live in the breath.

- Amit Ray, Om Chanting and Meditation

Signs of Anxiety from Overthinking

The signs of overthinking and the anxiety created by the process of overthinking are listed below. We will be taking a deeper look at each of these signs as we move through the book.

Warning Flags of Overthinking

Listed below are just some of the common signs you, or someone you know, maybe experiencing as a result of overthinking. We will be examining each of these signs in the coming chapters.

Worry Loop: A worry loop gets stuck in a person's head when a stressful situation occurs, and the person does not have the coping tools to deal with the problem. So instead of taking some kind of action, the person starts to think about the issue or situation until he or she is completely overwhelmed. All the possibilities and scenarios running through their head, looping through them over and over trying to figure out what will happen. This person wants to know all possible outcomes of a situation before you have to face it.

The Mean-Mouth Loop: This is the little voice that pops into people's heads reassuring them that they are not, and never will be good enough for that job, relationship, skill, team, or dance, etc. A recording of all the reasons they shouldn't try because they know their efforts will end in failure.

Lack of Sleep: Insomnia is common amongst people who overthink. They wake up after a couple of hours of sleep and the loops start. Their mind starts racing. How is that presentation going to go tomorrow? What I'm I going to do about earning more income? What if he/she shows up at the event? And as they start running through the familiar scenarios. Then the Mean-Mouth Loop kicks in to add to their distress.

Analysis Loop: People who find themselves remembering certain conversations word for word. They turn that conversation over and over in their head analyzing what was said, what was meant, what was not said, what was said between the lines, what was not meant, what was meant between the lines. Then the Worry Loop kicks in to run scenarios and is soon joined by Mean-Mouth to tie each and every scenario up with a failed resolution.

Nothing in Moderation: People who overthink have a tendency to see the world as black and white or issues as right or wrong. They go all in every time and don't vet situations properly. This can lead to misunderstandings, hurt feelings, and anger. Which then leads to feelings of inadequacy and self-doubt that can fuel depression or anxieties?

Stressed Relationships: Overthinking can lead to friends and family distancing themselves. The over-thinker wants reassurance that they are smart, attractive, good at their chosen profession, witty, etc. In other words, everything their Mean-Mouth Loop is telling them that they are not. This can be overwhelming for the friend or spouse who doesn't understand what is going on and has no skills or tools to deal with the situation.

Blue or Black Moods: Overthinking leads to depressed moods if left unchecked. There are built-in recordings ready to kick off at a moment's notice telling a person how stupid and unattractive other people find. That's hard to take day after day.

Reasons and Meaning: What is the point of all this looping? To find a reason or meaning in everything. A wish to feel part of every event and gathering. The person has isolated his/herself so thoroughly (even though it is not apparent to friends and acquaintances) they crave love, attention, and a connection with the rest of the world.

Self-Medicating: All of this stress and anxiety can often lead to substance abuse as a means of numbing the pain and fears.

Fear of Failure: Failure one way in which people learn. While the first try didn't work, correct observed flaws and try again. But someone who is afraid of being laughed at or looking bad in the eyes of family members can stop taking a risk and trying new ideas. They may stop setting goals and end up paralyzed by fear. They can't make a decision to move on, so they stay put and get stuck.

Physical Effects: Overthinking can lead to body aches from being physically tense for long periods of time. Headaches and fatigue can result from lack of sleep and all the effort it takes to worry so much.

Counseling vs. Self-Help

Whether you choose to counsel to work through a problem or self-help tools, both paths can be beneficial. Obviously, the self-help route is less expensive. Usually, it consists of a few books, your time, and maybe an art or yoga class. But don't rule out counseling if you find self-help is not getting to the root of the matter. I can't say this enough, **speak with your physician and let him or her guide you to find the help you need.**

What is counseling like?

Basically, it is the counselor's job to get you talking and then listen very closely to what you say. They can determine quite a lot by the way you phrase things. Then they will ask you questions about your answers. It's kind of like peeling an onion away layer by layer. In the middle is the root of the problem.

There are a variety of specialists in counseling depending on the type of trauma you might be experiencing. This is why it's a good idea to talk to your physician for a referral. General counseling for basic emotional stresses, couples, grief, and childhood traumas are some of the specialty counselors available. Sessions are usually about fifty minutes in length.

It is similar to talking with a close friend, but a counselor will point thinks out, gently, that a friend might not feel comfortable discussing. It can be painfully obvious from what a friend is saying that her husband is having an affair. But it is equally obvious that your friend is in denial about the situation. You could bluntly put two and two together for her, but you will make her feel worse than she already feels. There is also a distinct possibility that the information would end your friendship.

With a counselor the client can say whatever they need to without worrying about losing a friend; shaming their family, or revealing information they were asked to keep confidential. The counselor can point out an issue that might upset the client, but that is the counselor's job and again there is no worry of an ended friendship or feeling of betrayal of trust or other stressors that go along with friends and secrets.

This is not a one size fits all solution. You may not click with your counselor and need to find another. There is no specified time frame for figuring out your problem. What is certain, the more you open up and talk to the counselor, the sooner the problem will be solved. Don't hide issues. You will only hurt yourself and waste your own time and money.

~ Successful people have fear, successful people have doubts, and successful people have worried. They just don't let these feelings stop them. ~

- T. Harv Eker

Building Confidence

No matter which path you choose, the goal of self-help or counseling is to gain the skills you need to navigate life's difficult stress-filled situations. These skills are often termed Coping Strategies and will be discussed at greater length in chapter 4. You want to feel that you are capable of handling whatever comes your way. Positive feelings and confidence should grow as a result of your hard work. You should also see a support network start to form around you and realize that you are a part of other's support network.

How do you build confidence?

Completion of Task - When you complete a task or achieve a goal, you feel better about yourself. You know you can rely on yourself to get things done in a timely manner. This gets noticed by others and you begin to build a reputation as a reliable person.

Measuring Goals - Big or small, it is always a good idea to break goals down into manageable parts. As you complete each step you build confidence knowing that you are on schedule and on your way to completion of the goal. Even if the unexpected happens, you have a plan, so you can adjust your steps and still know you are going to reach your goal.

Do what You Love - Make time to take care of yourself. No matter what you love: music, outdoor sports, good food & company to go with it, or walking with your pets. Make time in your schedule to do what you love. After all, that's why you are working so hard.

Have Integrity - When you are faced with a tough decision and maybe not in your best interest to follow through with the task you promised to complete. Do the right thing and complete the task. Not only is it character building, but it also defines you as a person of your word, which is priceless. You are someone people can depend upon.

Take Risk - Don't bite off more than you can chew but do plan out those wonderful goals and go for it. And when it feels like you have taken on too much and you are overwhelmed by the project, afraid of failure, dig deep and carry on. Shove the fear aside and follow your plan.

Don't Back Down - Don't let the naysayer's stop you from getting what you want. When you don't get support from someone you thought would be rooting for you, don't let the doubt seep into your feelings. Keep on your path and you will show them.

Sometimes we deal with a difficult situation by burying it deep down or sweeping it aside as if it were "nothing" or "handled." If you find this is the case as you work the exercises in this book, you might want to add some counseling to your action plan. The incident could have been the death of a family member or friend, some trauma that happened long ago, or the loss of a job. No matter what it was, it still hurts and you might need someone to help you through the grieving process so that you can move on with your life.

Route, self-help or counseling, start with these exercises in this book. By the time you finish, you will have the tools to track your changes and see if you are making progress. This will allow you and your physician to determine you might benefit from some other therapies. Don't withhold information on issues and situations that concern you. Without all the pieces, it takes longer to solve the puzzle. Only you can make your therapy a success through hard work and change.

Chapter 2: Positive Thinking Vs. Positive

Speaking

Most people usually mistake both terms to mean the same when in actual sense they are different, although they both stem from the same principles.

Positive thinking like I had earlier explained has a wider scope in comparison to positive speaking. Positive thinking has more to do with our outlook of life and the environment where we live, than positive speaking does. Although they go hand in hand, where without one, the other might be incomplete and not genuine. Both concepts are a reaction to both internal and external factors, used to repel negativity, and negative occurrences.

Positive thinking is a mental and emotional tool that is employed to help you set your focus on the bright side of life, and to always expect that positive things will result from the things you do.

Meanwhile, positive speaking is simply the use of language in communicating our positive thoughts. It is very possible to have positive thinking as a habit and still be negative in speech. The more reason they are not the same. Some people, for the fear of being seen as too optimistic and imbalanced, mistaken as being proud, the fear of open disappointments or from lack of sufficient self-esteem decide to just internalize their positivity, so they think it, but don't speak it. But then, there is never a complete positive attitude without positive speaking, it is one of the most important and difficult tools in allaying fears, anxiety and negativity.

The singular step of adjusting the structure of your speech can be the factor that will make all the difference and bring the things that you desire the most, close to you.

If not for yourself, for the ones that you claim to love, develop the right speech etiquettes. Your speech is powerful. If you have not noticed, please realize today that your speech is powerful. You can influence other people's lives with the fruit of your lips. So when you constantly tell a friend that he sucks at something, he'll eventually believe that he does. Remember that your continual, negative projection of another person's reality could hinder that person's improvement, so positive speaking is not only good for us, but for those around us too.

So below is an exercise that you can take to help yourself out of negative speaking.

First, to decipher your need for this exercise, try this out for a week. Consciously track your pattern of speech. If you like, you could go around with a voice recording device to keep track of your speech pattern, and your mostly used words. Now note that positive thinking is not about the individual words you say, but the aura you communicate when you react to an occurrence through speech. After recording all week, take out time to analyze your data. Below are the parameters you should look out for:

Does my speech project hope more than bleakness?

Does my speech help people believe more in themselves or in their ideas?

Do people have beaming aura after speaking to me?

Do people see more possibilities when I speak?

If you answered no to most of the questions, then you should go on with reading this. You can cultivate positive speaking habits by going through the following guidelines:

Negative phrases should be substituted with a more positive phrase in its place. Take a look at the table below

Negative words	Positive words
I feel confused	I am not thinking clearly
I feel awful	I kind of feel out of sorts today

I'm getting tired	I need a rest
You are weird	You are different
I am going to be late again	I wish I could be on time
I hate him	I dislike him
She failed	She was unsuccessful
That is bad	That is improper
She is a troublesome child	She is an active child

Another thing to do is that, before sending replies, cross examine what you are about to say more often in your speech.

Note that you can only get the best out of positive speaking by making it a lifestyle. Because the rate at which you rid yourself of all your negative speech patterns is as fast as they can return.

Today, make a resolve to learn how to develop positive thinking and a positive speaking toward yourself, the people around you and even your life.

Chapter 3: Identify Your Worries And Deal

With Them

Are you plagued by worries? Do you lay awake at night thinking about problems and overthinking certain aspects of your life? You are not alone, everyone has concerns and worries but it is how you deal with them that is important. There are certain things that life is just too short to worry about.

How to deal with problems that we all face

1) Finances: as the saying goes the only guarantees in life are death and taxes. That doesn't mean you should let either worry you so much that you lose sleep. Bills and money are both things that need to be addressed but here are a few tips to help you deal with them in a calm and sensible way:

●Create a personal budget based on your income and your outgoings. Seeing your details in black and white will help you cut back on any unnecessary spending and review your finances.

•Cut any bills that are "luxury" If your income isn't stretching enough to pay for unessential bills then you need to cut them. Cable tv is not essential, neither is Amazon Prime, Netflix or other prime entertainment options. There is a plethora of entertainment options to choose from that are free.

•Prioritize your debts: Payback any outstanding loans to family and friends and avoid resentment. Debts to utility companies and banks can be negotiated but your friends and family will always be there for you when you need them.

•Pay your mortgage/rent: Keeping a roof over your head is the main concern. Your car and other concerns can wait.

2) The Past: History is an interesting subject but sometimes we can be haunted by our own personal history. The past is important, but it cannot be changed. What has happened is in the past and should not

be a burden that affects your future. The only way you can be affected by your history is if you let it happen.

3) Negative influences: Social media and the world of "celebrity culture" has given rise to a new brand of human beings. "Haters" are all around us, people who believe they are entitled to say whatever they like about whoever they choose. Haters are not just concerned with famous people and chances are you will encounter negativity from people daily. If you let their attitude and comments affect you and cause you to stress you will never achieve anything. Don't stress the haters! Gossips are also a scourge on society and should be treated as such. It is great to talk with friends and family about their lives and what is going on with them but when they share details of other people's personal details it is time to walk away. Nobody trusts a gossip; they often have a negative destructive effect and rarely have a good word for anyone.

4) Aging: Getting old is scary. In your mind, you still feel like a youngster, but the mirror tells a different story! However, there is nothing you can do about it and you are going to age no matter what. Stop worrying about your impending journey into old age and instead embrace it. Accept the laughter lines and grey hairs and stop wishing you were younger, do fun things that you couldn't do in your youth and make the most of your time on earth. If you are still young and wish you were older then you must stop wishing your life away and make the most of your youth!

5) Death: The Grim Reaper is a figure that represents the inevitability of your impending death and cannot be dodged. Stop worrying about your mortality and what happens after you die and start living life to the full.

6) F.O.M.O.: The fear of missing out is a constant worry for some people and can ruin their social life. Social media allows us

an unprecedented view of other people's activities and can lead to us convincing ourselves we are missing out on something. Stop worrying about what others are doing and walk your own path. Nobody else is going to pay your bills and put food on your table so focus on yourself.

7) What if's: Have you ever said something like this "What if I go to the store today and there is a robbery, and someone gets shot"? "What if I break down in the car and get stranded". If fear keeps you from doing anything you need to start acting and stop procrastinating. Fear is difficult to conquer but you need to realize that no matter how well you plan stuff there is a chance it may go wrong. This should not stop you from doing it!

8) Mistakes: If someone tells you they never make mistakes then they are lying to you. Fact. Nobody's perfect and the trick is to learn from your mistakes, figure out what caused it and improve the way

you do things in the future. Making a string of mistakes can be frustrating and disheartening but if you let these feelings affect you the idea of failure will overwhelm you. Clear your mind and reconsider the task in hand, ask advice if needed and start with a fresh slate.

9)   Anything beyond your control: Do you find yourself getting annoyed by things that are out of your control? Do you get aggravated by the weather, traffic and natural disasters? Just ask yourself why! You can have a measure of control over these things but merely your own perception and attitude. Reduce your stress levels and focus on things that are pertinent to your life. The weather will be the same even if you aren't worried about it so carry on with the task in hand and just let nature get on with it.

10)   Perfection: We all want to be the best version of ourselves, but we all have flaws. Accept that your faults are part of your make up and stop wasting your time trying

to be perfect. If you fill your life with stuff that makes you feel fulfilled and happy you will soon realize that having a perfect life is not your goal. A happy life is much more fulfilling and even mistakes can be fun!

If your life is stuck in neutral, try sitting down and clearing your mind for 10 minutes. Close your eyes and picture yourself in a restful place, the beach, your favorite chair or even floating in a warm bath. Whatever relaxes you? Drop all the "problems" in your life from your mind and remember, life is too short to worry about.........

Chapter 4: The Futility And Fatality Of

Worry

In life, worry is easily one of the most pointless emotions there is. Frankly, if given critical thought, it would be discovered that worry is without a purpose, and nothing can be gained from it. So, regardless of how much work is put into it, nothing can be expected of it. Worry is simply a futile indulgence. As a matter of fact, even an emotion as dreaded as fear serves more purpose than worry. Worry involves expecting that something can go wrong — something that would upset your desires and tilt the scales. But if you can take a moment to really think about the whole point of worrying, you will discover there is no point to it. As a matter of fact, absolutely nothing can be solved by worrying about it. Worry can't be used as a solution, and it most definitely doesn't elicit anything positive. So, if anything, worry compounds your woes and leaves you feeling miserable for yourself.

In worrying, we give thoughts to everything beside the present. We think about the future and what could come of it until we are helplessly overwhelmed by negative thoughts. For instance, when driving by a long vehicle, you are worried that its cargo might come undone and smash into your vehicle. Sure, that's a possibility all right, but why put your time and effort into thinking about probabilities when you could just drive on? Instead of dwelling in the moment, and keeping yourself focused on your driving, you choose to spend that moment envisioning an unlikely happenstance. Now, give it a thorough thought: how did worrying about something change anything? When has anything you worried about ever come to fruition?

By worrying, you don't do yourself any favors. No. And the intriguing thing about worrying is how it seems to make us feel connected — like you are doing yourself a favor by giving cognizance to future probabilities. In the end, you feel like your worries are somehow relevant, because they seem completely relative to your desires and fears and concerns. But know this: just because you worry about your grades, or if you'll get promoted, or if the person next door likes you back, or if you will ever make history, or if you will ever be good enough, doesn't make anything better. No. It neither changes the future nor tweaks the past. You are simply crying over spilt milk — and nothing can be done about it.

Thinking about what is yet to happen is a pointless indulgence. Worrying about the standard of a house doesn't make it more likely to cave in. All worry does is to preoccupy your mind and steal you from the present. And that's basically all it can do. What's worse is how we have grown to perceive worry as a necessity for human survival. Worry has been so integrated into our culture that it's become the norm, and one who doesn't worry as much is considered carefree or careless. Truth be told, those who don't worry are the happiest and lead the best lives. Worrying about the past, present, or future doesn't altogether make them right. You only lose the energy and happiness you need to live a happy life. Fear is fed and anxiety is groomed, but nothing changes about what you worry about. Another intriguing thing about worrying is how extremely easy it is to do. All you need do is give cognizance to something, and half a negative thought later, you're well on your way to worrying about it.

But if worrying is half as bad as we say it is, why do we still indulge in it?

Easy enough. We worry for a variety of reasons; some inane, others slightly reasonable, but pointless altogether. We worry because people worry. We worry because it has become engraved in our culture, and carelessness is the new tag for a worry-free life. We worry because we constantly engage in repetitive negative thinking. We worry because, somehow, we feel reinforced by constantly thinking about a particular thing. We worry because worry is limitless, and once begun can become habitual. That is, the more we worry, the more we are less likely to not worry. Being anxious of outcomes makes us worry, and in worrying, we develop anxiety. This is how complicated a loop worrying gets us into. Worrying boils down to overthinking things and the confusion of imagining worrying as being caring or cautious. If we can maintain mindfulness of the present, we can successfully free ourselves from the grasp of worry. You have to understand that you can't change an outcome by worrying about it. You have to be in the here and now to plan for and change the outcome of things. That is the only way anything ever works, and that's the way to attain inner peace.

What Does Worrying Mean?

1. Worrying is an indication of overthinking:

When thinking grows into worrying, it has become futile. Keep this in mind. As humans, we think a lot. It is habitual. That is how we are programmed as thinking beings from infancy until our earliest development and then eventual death. But until we learn to not cross the thin line between basic thinking and overthinking and learn to ease up on our thoughts, we will end up worrying. We should all know this, but it turns out the ones who should've imparted us with the knowledge were themselves worriers. Don't get it wrong; being able to ponder things is a beautiful and powerful experience. Albeit, when you make a habit of it, it extends into everything, even the ones not worth the bother. You become used to ruminating about everything and anything so much so that you get tied into a loop. Ruminating now becomes regular and repetitive. And since we have such high tendencies of noticing things we think are undesirable, we end up thinking more about negative outcomes than positive ones. Even when much of that thinking is very unnecessary.

Deliberate and dedicated thinking is a necessary indulgence for when we want to plan. But anything aside it just flips the script. In the same way we notice all the negative things in our lives, we can unlearn that, choosing instead to notice all the positive thoughts which occur to us. In doing this, we dismiss the negative ones which give rise to worrying. In essence, we can learn to notice the things that give us joy — the great, wholesome, and practical thoughts. Although it's possible for practical thoughts to be negative in themselves, they become relevant and positive when they are related to practical matters and irrelevant otherwise. Thus, they aren't constantly used to fuel unnecessary and pointless worrying.

2. We worry about the time:

It is a common happenstance for us to constantly worry about time-related outcomes. We spend our time thinking about what was, could be, will be, or may be. And although these thoughts may have been triggered by real-time memories, it should be kept in mind that the reality remains much unchanged. Sure, our worrying about time is a form of brain activity, but it isn't our reality — not anymore at least. We should take them as past experiences to learn from, not ones to drown ourselves in. Our life happens and depends on the here and now, so it's time to get our heads out of the clouds. Nothing goes on outside the present, not the past nor the future. Whatever experiences we have had or will have, be it good or bad, and the memories they elicit, it is imperative to note that only the now counts. Anything else outside the present isn't material. It is mere thought whatever it is, bad or good memories, happy or dreadful anticipations — they are still all thoughts. Keep in mind that when we are fully absorbed by the present and dwell in it, even if momentarily, all our worries would vanish. At this point, we would have a real glimpse of reality where we are without worries and nothing else matters.

3. Confusing worrying with caring:

One of the most erroneous beliefs we take with us as we grow is believing that worrying means you care. This is not the case usually. Worrying is NOT caring. Let's consider the rationale behind it. If we think worrying is caring, as we often do, all we do is agree that it is impossible for us to show care without first worrying, and when we don't worry, we can't care. Having considered it in this light, can we still agree on that being the case? Surely not. In worrying, we stress ourselves out, and in doing this, we make others stress one way or the other.

A paradigm shift in this regard will let us see things in a different way: to care without having to worry, caring while breathing still. Refraining from worrying, as opposed to lack of care, results in a healthier life devoid of stress and mental strain. Does this connote an occasional and apparent absence of commitment to care? No. This is another point in which a paradigm shift is needed. Being careless and carefree are in themselves two distinct notions. Occasionally, it is imperative that they overlap as the result is healthy, joyful, and enthusiastic.

To summarize, take note of how frustrated you become when things are beyond your control. You tend to feel overwhelmed. However, somehow, we feel that worrying about something well beyond our control makes it any better or bearable. Ironical, isn't it? Worrying is pointless; it works you up and is nothing but unhealthy. Whatever way it is considered, and regardless of the form it takes, worrying is a counterproductive and utterly useless emotion which outputs nothing whatsoever. The best cause of action when we begin worrying is to turn our focus and channel our mental energy into doing what we can change. The logic is to act like children: forget about what you can't change. Like adults, they aren't without emotions of anger, unhappiness, or sadness. But every other time is a chance to start anew. Without grudges or baggage, they forget everything and just move on. To alter our method of thinking, we have to decipher that we have power over what we think about. Our thought habits are made up of anything we let enter our minds. For this reason, it is imperative that we practice living in the moment, refraining from letting out minds wander, and learn to let our minds be at rest. But most important of all, we have to be in the present. Make plans for the future all you want, but don't get caught in a daydream. Learn from the past, unlearn how to worry, and just leave what isn't at that. Having nothing to worry about beats worrying about anything any day.

4. We worry about future happenings:

Sometimes, we worry almost automatically. We don't plan for it, but we end up doing it anyway. Oftentimes, the reason for this lies in our innate desire to know what the future brings. Future outcomes are easily our greatest points of worrying. So, while we are stuck waiting for the future to come to us, we engage ourselves in the present by worrying. It also happens that when we find ourselves in positions where a call to action is required, we freak out with worry from indecisiveness and anxiety about taking the right course of action. Given the way our minds are wired, we are programmed to engage in one thing or another. The mind is never simply at a state of rest or totally devoid of thoughts at any one time. So, in the absence of being able to do anything about a situation, worrying becomes the next course of action for the blank and idle mind.

5. The fatality of worrying:

When we engage in a constant habit of worrying, we inhibit ourselves from achieving any creative solution and leave no room for positive thoughts. In this section, we will consider some of the fatalities of worrying.

Worrying to obsessive degrees can prove to be a rather stressful indulgence which can result in very serious health complications. Diseases such as constipation, heart problems, and nervous disorders, among others, are common occurrences in people who are continuously stressed from their habit of regularly indulging in worrying.

Worrying can lead to sleeplessness: A good many people will often worry from the very minute they hit the hay, usually because they can't indulge themselves in anything else until they fall asleep. However, worrying only makes the mind more stimulated, making it harder to fall asleep in the process. In turn, you will have higher chances of getting negative thoughts which beget bad sleeping patterns and a lack of proper sleep.

Lack of concentration: When you are caught up worrying about things, it is quite a challenge to maintain concentration on any given task. If duly considered, it can be noted that those who spend their time worrying are less likely to produce optimal performance and will typically exude an obvious lack of quality in their endeavors.

Worrying is detrimental to health: Constantly worrying about things can make you susceptible to a vast range of health issues. These issues would typically include but not be limited to the following: colds, sleep disorders, poor appetite, itches, coughing, constipation, wheezing, indigestion, and headaches.

Worrying deprives you of clarity: Repetitively thinking about things tends to weigh down your cognition over time, leading to loss of clarity in thinking. When you tune your focus into worrying about a specific problem, you will fail to recognize a solution even when one comes your way.

Chapter 5: What Are The Symptoms Of

Overthinking?

From time to time, we all become consumed by a problem or situation which we can't stop thinking about. When that happens, there is no choice but to try and manage our feelings as best we can.

Here are some clear signs that demonstrate you may be going through an overthinking episode:

A basic quality of overthinkers is that they see the world in high contrast. This means that everything that happens is a tragedy.

They are always thinking about the worst-case scenario even when it isn't even close to being that bad.

They crave for affection, yet they don't always get it. Often, overthinking is just a ploy to get attention. While this isn't always the case, it might be worth asking yourself if it is just the comfort that you seek.

They pay attention to others' assessments as well. Considering the opinions of others is crucial in understanding your feelings and what you can do about those issues which worry you.

Overthinking is often characterized by a pessimistic attitude. While it's perfectly normal to worry about things now and then, pathological overthinkers tend to be glass-half-empty folks.

These individuals may turn into a burden to their closest friends and family. This is especially true if overthinkers are unable to function properly in their usual, day to day activities.

An overthinker attempts to locate importance in all things. Indeed, everything is urgent, everything is a life and death struggle, and everything is headed toward a tragic end.

You are overthinking if something is at the forefront of your thoughts and you persistently go over it. If you find yourself that you can't let something go, chances are you are simply overthinking things.

Experience the ill effects of sleep deprivation. It is common for overthinkers to lose sleep on a regular basis. While it's normal when you have something important to worry about, the chronic overthinker will experience sleep deprivation issues as a result of their pathological worrying.

Overthinkers recollect each and every word and detail from a discussion. If you find yourself keeping a play by play account of your conversations, then there is a very good chance you fall under the category of overthinkers.

Overthinkers have trouble relating to others. These folks will find it hard to build lasting relationships especially if they are bent in seeing the worst of every situation. So, if you happen to find yourself overly concerned about things, worrying excessively, or simply losing sleep on a consistent basis, perhaps it's time to look inward and find out what is really at the root of your overthinking tendencies.

Chapter 6: Anxiety

Anxiety occurs as a result of stress. It presents itself in the body as a feeling of fear about the future. This is especially true when we feel that a future event is out of our control. It can also be true if an event is something we fear doing. For example, many people will experience anxiety before doing some form of public speaking.

While everyone experiences anxiety from time to time, an anxiety disorder may exist when these feelings persist for long periods without going away. When they become inhibiting to your everyday life, it may be because you are suffering from some form of anxiety disorder.

Anxiety disorders can feel similar to the fleeting feelings of anxiety most people get from time to time but the difference is that they often stay with the person for much longer. Some people live in a constant state of anxiety and others can get very severe bouts of anxiety which leads to panic attacks.

If anxiety disorders are not dealt with, they can prevent a person from enjoying life's pleasures and the constant state of stress experienced by the body can also lead to many chronic illnesses such as heart disease.

Types of anxiety disorder

There are many different types of anxiety disorder by they all tend to stem from a fear of some future occurrence. They include:

•Phobias - this is an (often irrational) fear of a particular thing

•Separation anxiety disorder - this is the fear of being separated from those close to you
•Social anxiety disorder - this is the fear of other people's opinions about you in social scenes
•Panic disorder - this is when someone experiences panic attacks at irregular intervals
•Illness anxiety disorder - people suffering from this disorder used to be referred to as hypochondriacs. It is when you are anxious about your health
•Obsessive-compulsive disorder - this is when you must do things in a certain way in fear that doing it a different way will lead to an undesired result.

Symptoms of anxiety

There is a range of different feelings and emotions experienced by people when they are suffering from anxiety. People experience anxiety in different ways, but the main reported symptoms include:
•Difficulty to concentrate

- Increased levels of breathing and heart rate
- Inability to rest
- Symptoms of an anxiety attack
- Anxiety attacks can be very frightening experiences for both the individual having the attack and other people present. An attack may come as a result of anxiety that has been building for a while. Again, the symptoms experienced by people may differ but many of the common symptoms are:
- Sweating
- Rapid breathing
- Dizziness
- Chills
- Severe worry and fear
- Tingling sensations
- Numbness

Causes of anxiety

There is no definitive evidence to exactly what causes anxiety to occur but it is likely due to a number of combining factors. Some factors are a result of an individual's brain chemistry, as well as their environment and genetics.

It is also believed that the brain area corresponding with fear plays a role. This is known as the amygdala and it is part of the limbic system of the brain which controls fear, anxiety and other emotional responses.

The prefrontal cortex is the area of the brain that is responsible for conscious thought and rational thinking. It is believed that anxiety occurs in individuals when the connection between the prefrontal cortex and the amygdala is not sufficiently strong. Therefore, when something seems threatening to the body, the conscious mind cannot communicate effectively to tell the body that everything is ok. For example, you may have an exam coming up that you haven't studied for. While you know logically that failing the exam is not a threat to your livelihood, your prefrontal cortex is unable to explain this to the amygdala who is now causing you to experience severe anxiety about the exam.

Anxiety treatments

While some doctors may prescribe drugs to help you deal with anxiety, often a change in lifestyle is all that is needed. In very bad situations, however, a person may need some extra treatment to help them get by from day-to-day.

There are often two methods prescribed for those needing serious treatment. The first type of treatment involves medication in the form of sedatives and antidepressants. These help to alter the chemicals in the brain to bring them back to levels where stress is reduced. Another approach is to use psychotherapy in order to learn and develop the tools you need to deal with anxiety when it happens.

There are also alternative activities that have proven to be very useful in reducing anxiety. It often takes a person to proactively take care of their mind and body. Beneficial activities include:

- Meditation
- Consuming less caffeine and alcohol
- Exercising regularly
- A healthy, balanced diet
- Getting good quality sleep

Anxiety is common

It is important to realize that anxiety is a problem that many people face. Do not think you are somehow weak or abnormal for experiencing anxiety. It is most likely due to an imbalance in the brain and with some work, it can be rectified. It is important to accept that you have anxiety in order for you to deal with it. Trying to push it away and deny it won't help. You must understand why it is happening and search for the triggers that cause you to feel anxiety.

Anxiety triggers

Everyone has different situations that trigger their anxiety and sometimes anxiety seems to manifest for no reason at all. It is important to take stock of what triggers your anxiety so you can know what to avoid. In most cases, however, people experience many of the following as triggers:

●Health problems: Many people experience anxiety after discovering they have health issues. This is understandable as the initial shock of a health issue may trigger the fear response.

●Medicines: Certain medicines such as the morning-after pill have been known to trigger anxiety

●Coffee: Caffeine can play a role in triggering anxiety as it increases the body's chance of stress

●Low blood sugar: If you haven't eaten enough food you may experience low blood sugar which can cause anxiety. Your body goes into a fearful state because it is not receiving all the nutrients it expects.

●Negative thoughts: When you have negative thoughts about yourself or the future, your body can sense this and fear may kick in.

•Financial concerns: When people worry about money and savings, or their job stability, anxiety can be triggered.

•Social events and parties: People suffering from social anxiety may panic when in a room full of strangers.

•Conflict: Problems in your relationships or other disagreements may trigger anxiety.

How Depression relates to Anxiety

Anxiety and depression tend to be closely linked. Many people suffering from anxiety are also suffering from depression. Anxiety can stem as a result of depression and also the other way around. Depression can also be tackled with many of the same treatments as anxiety with lifestyle changes being one of the most fundamental aspects of the process.

Anxiety in kids

Many children now experience anxiety. This is a new phenomenon that is becoming concerning as anxiety is not a natural state of mind for young people. Children usually live in a much more present state than adults as they discover the world around them. One of the reasons that anxiety in children is on the rise is most likely due to the increase in their use of technology in the form of smartphones and tablets. Anxiety comes as a result of worrying about the future and the use of technology can often disconnect us from the present as we compare our lives to others on social media.

Other people's opinions

When I was younger, my mind was always racing with thoughts about everything. Mostly though, these thoughts consisted of what other people's opinions of me might be. Ironically, other people's opinions are one of the few things in life we have no control over yet many of us spend much of our days worrying about them.

We must forgive ourselves for this, however, as worrying about what other people close to us think about us was very important in early human societies. For thousands of years, humans existed in tribes of no more than 150 individuals. For tribes to work and cooperate successfully, there needed to be a certain degree of trust amongst the tribe members. If some members of the tribe didn't like you for some reason, you were at risk of being excommunicated from the tribe. This would have resulted in almost certain death as you no longer had the protection the tribe brought or the access to food that would have been foraged and hunted in groups. This led humans to develop a strong need to be socially connected and also a fear of being not liked or different from others in fear of being isolated from the tribe.

While nowadays we don't necessarily need the protection of a tribe for survival, we still have the same innate urge to impress others and hope that they like us. Being liked by most people still serves us well in today's world. If you have a likable character you will tend to do better in areas of life such as business, friendships, and intimate relationships.

However, when you focus directly on your reputation or what other people think of you, it tends to lead to a lot of stress as you become less decisive about your actions. Instead of doing what you feel is right, you act in a way that you think the other person would prefer you to act. This leads to constant mental clutter as you try to rethink every instinctive action from the view of the other person. When you are interacting with numerous people this becomes even more difficult as you have to find the common ground where you can be likable by all.

Instead of focusing on your reputation and what other people might think of you based on what you say or do, focus on your character and the values and principles that you believe in. Act in accordance with these values and principles instead of through the imagined lens of others and you will live a much more stress-free life. You will no longer have to worry about the opinions of others because those who you should want to be socially connected with will be able to see your core values and principles through your actions. If they also have similar beliefs, they will resonate well with you. You will not have to deal with the mental clutter that comes as a result of acting against your impulses. You will be able to listen to your instinct more and you won't have to second-guess all of your actions. This will free up your mind for the more important things in your life that you could spend time contemplating.

Chapter 7: Taking Control Of Your

Thoughts

2.1 Panic Attacks and Stress Response
As humans, we have this response called the "Fight or Flight" response, a physiological reaction to whatever our body considers life-threatening or dangerous.

This response is also referred to as acute stress response and it shares the same reactions or feelings such as shaking anxiety and fear that occurs when our body is preparing for a possible emergency. The alternative to the "Fight or Flight" response is the body's relaxation response. This is known as the recovery period is the body's way of normalizing its functions. This happens between 20 to 60 minutes after the perceived threat disappears.

Why Do We Have the "Fight or Flight" Response?

Our "Fight or Flight" response is a result of stress, and this is something that stemmed from the survival mode from our early ancestors who lived in dangerous times. For example, prehistoric cavemen were in constant danger of animals. One minute they might be lighting a fire and the next minute, there's a stampede coming their way full of mammoths. The human design then kicks in and we have a full surge of energy and strength to quickly respond to the threat by removing ourselves from danger and increasing our chances of survival.

"Fight or Flight" Response with Panic Disorder

To some researchers, this old stress reaction is a continuation associated with modern-day panic disorders and this can be something like being afraid of large or small spaces or being in situations that are dark or no easy escape route.

What Happens When the Response Is Triggered?

Numerous physiological changes have been identified by researchers that happen when the "Fight or Flight" response takes place. When this happens, our bodies are triggered to prepare for the muscular activity that is required to fight or flee the danger.

Some of the changes that take place during this process include:

An Increased heart rate

Rapid breathing

Dilation of blood vessels to the muscles

Constriction of blood vessels to some parts of our body

Dilation of pupils

Tunnel vision

Auditory exclusion

Sweating

These changes occur instantly and if you were experiencing a life-threatening event, you would expect to feel of these physical occurrences happening to your body. However, if you suddenly feel like this when you're quietly having dinner or even grocery shopping, this is something to be looked into. In our modern time's stress is more due to psychosocial reasons but if you do get physical stress occurring all the time, then it could be detrimental.

Having Fear When There Is No Danger

When a person experiences a panic attack, the body's system is triggered without the presence of any visible signs of danger. It is the lack of or the absence of danger that greatly magnifies fear.

If there is no danger but a person begins to sweat, breathing and heart rate becomes rapid, we lose sight or sense of hearing, a person begins to fear the symptoms and even believe that they are life-threatening. Your body is telling you to get ready physically and that you are in grave danger but what about the psychological aspects for dangers that you cannot see? Experiencing these thoughts does not get you out of danger- they only strengthen and reinforce your association with fear and it is not based on the actual threat.

2.2 The Benefits of Relaxation

Relaxation can be anything but it is a state where you feel at peace and calm and you are able to manage your day-to-day life. It can be difficult to relax when you have a busy life but practicing it even in small ways can help you manage anxiety and stress.

Improving Mental Health with Relaxation

Stress and other mental health symptoms such as schizophrenia, depression, and anxiety are reduced when we relax and do plenty of relaxation habits and techniques throughout the day. Apart from that, we also experience many other benefits that are not immediately seen which are:

Lowering blood pressure

Lowered breathing rate

Lowered heart rate

Mood improvements and better concentration

Less anger and frustration

Confidence boost

Ability to rationally solve problems

Types of Relaxation Techniques

There are various kinds of relaxation techniques that you can try to manage stress and anxiety. Doctors, health practitioners, health care professionals as well as psychotherapists offer different methods based on the patient's needs and their line of knowledge.

You can also administer relaxation techniques on your own to refocus your attention on calming and increasing awareness of your body. It doesn't matter what kind of technique you choose so long as you feel comfortable doing it and you practice it regularly to reap its benefits.

Usually, relaxation techniques prescribed by therapists and doctors usually fall into these categories:

Types of relaxation techniques include:

Autogenic relaxation- this means something that comes from inside you. Using this relaxation technique requires the use of your visual imagery as well as your bodily awareness. With this technique, you repeat affirmations and words that help you reduce muscle tension as well as help you relax. You can imagine a peaceful setting and then focus your mind and relax your breathing. Meditation is one such technique that uses autogenic relaxation.

Progressive muscle relaxation- this relaxation technique requires you to focus on slowly tensing each group of muscles. Through this technique, it helps you be more focused on the difference between relaxation and muscle tensions. You begin by tensing and relaxing the muscles in your toes and then systematically work your way up to the neck and finally to the head. You can also begin from your head to the toes, tensing your muscles for 5 seconds and then relax for 30 seconds. Through this way, you can become more aware of physical sensations.

Visualization- This technique requires some form of mental visualization that is a journey towards a calming, peaceful and serene space or situation. You may need to incorporate as many senses as you can when relaxing with visualization and this could be the sense of smell, touch, and sound. If your relaxing space is on a beach, then you need to visualize the water, the ocean, the waves, and the sand. You would be required to sit or lie down comfortably in a quiet spot in order to visualize with no interruption, with your eyes closed and concentrate fully on your breathing.

Other relaxation techniques may include:

Hydrotherapy

Aromatherapy

Deep breathing

Massage

Yoga

Biofeedback

Music and art therapy

Meditation

Tai chi

Remember that relaxation takes practice. As you incorporate more and more relaxation techniques, you will learn to become more aware of the physical sensations related to stress as well as your muscle tension. When you are aware of what stress responses feel like, you can make a conscious effort to practice techniques of relaxation that can bring you back to a relaxed mode especially if you feel stress or panic symptoms creeping up. This will help you from allowing your stress reactions from spiraling out of control.

Relaxation Takes Time and Patience

As with any skill, you learn, developing proper relaxation techniques require practice, time and patience. You need to be patient with yourself and do not let this effort become another stressor. If one type of technique does not work for you, don't worry- try something else but never resort to unhealthy habits. Instead, talk to your doctor or healthcare provider for more options.

Some people with more serious psychological issues or history of trauma and abuse may experience some emotional discomfort when they go through relaxation techniques and if you do experience this, stop whatever you are doing and talk to your doctor.

2.3 Understanding Triggers of Your Anxiety

Identify Triggers

A large part of the prevention of anxiety is having an awareness of what causes it. Learning to identify your anxious thoughts when they come up can help you control and reduce them quickly. Awareness of your anxiety can help you identify the trigger and it can help you understand how it affects your feelings and behaviors. Once you understand the source of your fears or worries, you will have a clearer idea of how to relieve it.

Triggers are sometimes very clear. It could be a big presentation coming up, a major examination, or waiting on a result of something you have wanted for a long time. Once you know what triggers anxiety in you, you will be able to take steps to cope and help reduce the level of anxiety before it escalates.

For instance, if you are able to identify that your trigger for anxiety is exhaustion from juggling work and parenting, you can come up with a schedule to set aside time for each in advance. Be reasonable with yourself and set a realistic schedule that you can stick to. Through this, you would be able to spend time on both according to your priority.

If you know that your common stressor is the result of procrastination, you can start with pacing yourself and sticking to a plan that helps you reduce the bottleneck at the last minute.

Having a journal to record your moods, thoughts and predetermined stressors may also help you better identify triggers.

You may be able to stop lingering in futile thoughts that could increase your anxiety.

Always remember that you need to first take care of yourself before you are able to take care of others. Set aside some leisure time for yourself to relax your mind so that you are able to reduce the number of anxiety triggers.

2.4 Teaching Your Mind to Stop Overthinking

We all overthink sometimes especially when we want something to go right or we put in a lot of effort into it and we want to make it work out. Or even when we are getting ready for a vacation and we overthink about the security of our home or if we packed all the things we need. It happens. However, overthinking may be something you want to train your brain to reduce or stop doing if it starts disrupting life for you.

If all your overthinking leads towards an increase in anxiety or being pessimistic about everything, then it might cause you to stop the things you are doing simply because you think it would fail. Or if your overthinking prevents you from getting things done because you are too hung up on the negative aspects to focus and come up with a solution.

For chronic worriers, overthinking can cause negative consequences. It can also prevent us from enjoying the moment and instead, keep us fixated on future uncertainties that make us anxious and worried when we lack control.

Now let's look into the ways we can all train our brains to stop overthinking and look at the more positive aspects or even try to rationalize things so our reactions do not go out of control. We shall look into research conducted by a team of researchers from the University of California, Santa Barbara. They showed images of the colors of the kaleidoscope to study participant's reactions and looked into their ability to remember if they had seen any of these images before.

Participants who gave their best guess did better than those who spent time trying to remember the colors and patterns. In other words, the over thinkers did less well than those who did not focus their attention on remembering the details.

The team of researchers concluded that paying attention can sometimes be a distraction and also affect performance outcomes. Paying more attention to details hurt a person's ability to remember what they had seen.

So with that in mind, let's look at how we can train our brains to stop overthinking.

Train your brain to see the big picture

The research conducted by the team from the University of California shows that when it comes to recalling especially recalling complex images, a broad overview approach is better. In order to train your brain to process information using this method, you need to imagine taking all the various details at once, the same way your brain looks at a photo and all the different pieces of details at once. This is called under thinking and you can practice it by looking at picture books, opening random pages and looking at an image for 5 seconds. Next, close the book and try to recall everything you saw without spending too much time trying to remember. You will be surprised at how much you can recall because the short amount of time prevents your brain from overthinking. Repeat this exercise often till you feel confident in your brain's ability to process information rapidly.

Train your brain to be comfortable with uncertainty

Things are not always going to work out the way you want it to. There will be things that you will know and can know and there are things that you may never know or come across. When it comes to overthinking, people who do this have somehow trained their brains to focus on the unknown instead of the known. They look into uncertainties and try to solve something they do not know. Some questions can be answered but for overthinkers, they tend to dwell on those that they cannot answer. To train your brain not to do this is to either seek answers from the source of the questions that you are overthinking or keep telling your brain that it is okay not to know the answer at all.

Train your brain on how to think

This kind of thinking is called meta-thinking where we think about how to think and to do this, it requires some form of self- observation. If you are reading this chapter and you already have concerns about your overthinking, you are already aware of your own negative self-thinking and pessimistic thought patterns. People who experience issues about overthinking usually have negative thoughts about themselves and this is all because of their own personal thoughts and not of others. Allowing your negative thoughts to take precedence but rejecting them as being an element of what we identify as 'self' is one such way of helping overthinkers.

In the Journal of Behavior Therapy, researchers found that MBCT or mindfulness-based cognitive therapy has helped people feel less negative emotions and more self-compassion about their overthinking. People who have undergone MBCT have experienced less stress related to their thoughts.

Find something you can control

If you find yourself overthinking because you feel like you need to gain control over something that is happening to you, focus your thoughts on a concrete action step that you can immediately take to gain some sense of control and composure. It can be as simple as writing down an issue that allows your brain to stop trying to remember the issue. It could even be making a phone call to someone you trust to help you refocus and rationalize your situation so you know what to do. It can even be putting your headphones to block out the noise so you can concentrate on an action step to take.

2.5 Exercise and Tips to Calm your Anxiety
Treatments for Anxiety

While it is hard to determine whether your anxiety is a medical problem or just a bad experience, treating anxiety early is always easier than when it gets worse over time.

You should get a medical opinion if:

Your anxiety is hampering in your daily life. This includes your work, school or social life

You feel the need to use substances such as alcohol or drugs to manage your anxiety

Your fear or worry feels out of your control

You are having suicidal thoughts

You have the tendency to self-harm

You strongly feel that your anxiety is caused by a serious mental health condition

Next, if you have decided that you need help, please see your general practitioner. He or she can assist in determining whether your anxiety is related to a health problem, or whether it is due to a common stressor. Once it is clear, they will be able to draw out the right treatment plan to help you deal with your anxiety.

If your fear or worry is not the outcome of a serious health condition, you may be referred to a mental health specialist; either a psychiatrist or a psychologist, depending on the seriousness of your condition. A psychiatrist is a licensed medical practitioner who is qualified to diagnose and treat mental health conditions with or without prescribed medications. A psychologist is a mental health professional who can diagnose and treat mental health conditions, but solely through counseling without medication.

It is vital to get treatment from a mental health provider that you are comfortable with and that you trust. Ask your doctor to refer you to a few and take the time to meet them. It is not unusual for it to take a few meetings with each to find the one that is suitable for you. A psychological evaluation will help your mental health provider to diagnose an anxiety disorder. This could look like a therapy session of one-on-one with your mental health provider asking you questions regarding your feelings and behaviors. They may also match your behaviors or symptoms to the criteria for anxiety disorders listed in the Diagnostic and Statistical Manual of Mental Disorders (DSM-V) to establish a diagnosis.

Prevention and Coping with Normal Anxiety

Experiencing anxiety with normal daily stressors and worries can sometimes be difficult to manage. Knowing relief strategies and steps can help alleviate normal anxiety experienced in everyday life to a more manageable level.

Identify Triggers

A large part of the prevention of anxiety is having an awareness of what causes it. Learning to identify your anxious thoughts when they come up can help you control and reduce them quickly. Awareness of your anxiety can help you identify the trigger and it can help you understand how it affects your feelings and behaviors. Once you understand the source of your fears or worries, you will have a clearer idea of how to relieve it.

Triggers are sometimes very clear. It could be a big presentation coming up, a major examination, or waiting on a result of something you have wanted for a long time. Once you know what triggers anxiety in you, you will be able to take steps to cope and help reduce the level of anxiety before it escalates.

For instance, if you are able to identify that your trigger for anxiety is exhaustion from juggling work and parenting, you can come up with a schedule to set aside time for each in advance. Be reasonable with yourself and set a realistic schedule that you can stick to. Through this, you would be able to spend time on both according to your priority.

If you know that your common stressor is the result of procrastination, you can start with pacing yourself and sticking to a plan that helps you reduce the bottleneck at the last minute.

Having a journal to record your moods, thoughts and predetermined stressors may also help you better identify triggers. You may be able to stop lingering in futile thoughts that could increase your anxiety.

Always remember that you need to first take care of yourself before you are able to take care of others. Set aside some leisure time for yourself to relax your mind so that you are able to reduce the number of anxiety triggers.

Take Care of your Body

Exercise has been proven to reduce stress hormones that affect mood. Incorporating exercise can help lessen anxiety when it is triggered. The act of exercising can also help you disengage from unhelpful thoughts.

Some foods are found to be helpful in reducing anxiety. Foods with high omega 3 fatty acids and probiotics like salmon, walnuts, yogurt, and flaxseed can help curb anxiety. On the other hand, foods that contain high amounts of fat, sugar, salt, and caffeine can lead to prolonged anxiety symptoms. Therefore, maintaining a healthy diet is fundamental in preventing anxiety.

The lack of sleep can also be a trigger for anxiety. However, anxiety could also be the cause of sleeplessness. This vicious cycle can be managed by taking some time to wind down before bed with calming activities or meditation. Instead of worrying about the next day or what you are afraid of forgetting, try penning things down and putting your thoughts at ease.

Have a Support System

Research shows that those who have a strong support system consisting of close friends or family are able to fight mental health issues better than those who are isolated. Having someone you can talk to and let out your worries could help prevent anxiety from overwhelming you. Find someone you can trust to be a listening ear and give you constructive feedback on your thoughts. Sometimes having a second opinion helps in scaling down the enormity of the problems perceived.

Sometimes scheduling time alone is not as effective as scheduling time with the company. If you feel like it is more helpful to you, set aside time with friends or family instead of being alone with your own thoughts.

Therapy services such as Cognitive Behavioral Therapy (CBT) have also helped with the prevention of anxiety from escalating to a diagnosable disorder. Having a professional aid to help curb anxiety could be a good prevention strategy.

Learn Relaxation Strategies

Take deep breaths. Deep breathing, have been shown to slow heart rate, lower blood pressure and reduce stress.

A directed mental visualization called guided imagery can lead to instant relaxation. Guided imagery involves imagining a place or thing that can evoke calmness and let your mind to zone in on the positive and relaxing thoughts.

Bottom line

Mindfulness is a state of awareness of the present. Mindfulness practice, meditation, and yoga allows you to be aware of your surroundings and helps you be in control over how you experience situations and how you react. Feeling like you are losing control and overwhelmed is a common symptom of anxiety. In the next few chapters, we will explore more on meditation specifically to target anxiety.

Chapter 8: Over Thinking Are You Always

In Your Own Head

Lately I have been thinking over business things an lot more than usual. I would run the same topics over and over in my mind. I thought that I was probably the only person in the world doing this that is, until I talked with an friend about it. I was comforted by the fact that I am not the only person who does this. Just learning about it helped me snap out of it, hopefully it will help you to.

I decided to write and book about over thinking, and let other people out there know that they are not alone. So, I did some research. What I found was a bit surprising to me. Did you know that the university of Michigan did a study on over thinking an few years ago? They found that women are much more likely to fall into over thinking than men. Alcohol and drug abuse is more common in people who over think. The study also found that over thinking can interfere with problem solving and can lead to depression and anxiety, sometimes quite severe cases.

The good news is, it is never too late to overcome over thinking. Life is made of millions of moments, but we live only one of these moments at a time. As we begin to change this moment we begin to change our lives.

Are you someone who tends to over think things? What exactly is over thinking.

Over thinking

Over thinking is negative thinking magnified to the point where one loses control and is overwhelmed by one's thoughts. Over thinking may be triggered by a simple concern about a job, weight or family, an argument, an innocent comment from an friend or colleague, or anything that made a person feel sad, anxious or angry.

Instead of resolving the issue in mind, or moving on to other things, however, over thinking gives rise to more and more negative thoughts, often unrelated to the original problem. Mood gets deeper and darker, and one becomes more and more angry, sad and worried. Thoughts go round and round until one concludes that the situation is hopeless and nothing can be done to improve it.

Anyway? According to the psychologists, who have done extensive research in this area, over thinking is "thinking too much, needlessly and passively. And, endlessly pondering the meanings, causes and consequences of your character, your feelings and, especially, your problems."

After all the hard work, this should be the time of year, when we finally stop fretting and start enjoying ourselves, But how do you stop those naggin. 'what if?' worries crowding back?

We all do it sometimes – worry about things we've said or done, analyze throwaway comments others have or spend hours dissecting the meaning of a particular email or letter. Almost without realizing it, we get sucked into a spiral or negative thoughts and emotions that steal our joy and enthusiasm. It's a pattern that some psychologists call over thinking. The initial thoughts lead to more negative thoughts, the questions to more questions. The over thinking becomes a cascade that ferments and builds, so that everything gets out of control. Get stuck in this negative cycle

that ferments and builds, so that everything gets out of control. Get stuck in this negative cycle and it can affect your life. It can also lead to some really bad decisions when relatively small issues becomes so blown out of proportion that you lose your perspective on them.

When we over think concentrating on what has happened in the past (future) we are destroying the moment we are in. You miss out on experiencing and enjoying the here and now of your life. Why do we do it? At the most basic level, the biology of our brain makes it easy to over think. Thoughts and memories do not just sit in our brains isolated and independent from each other they are woven together in intricate networks of associations. One result of all these complex interconnections is that thoughts concerning a certain issue in you life can trigger thoughts about other connected issues.

 Most of us have some negative memories worries about the future or concerns about the present. Much of the time we're probably not conscious of these negative thoughts. But when they come over us, even if it's just because the weather's dreary or because we drunk too much wine, it's easier to recall the negative memories and begin the cycle of over thinking. Many women are overloaded with juggling home and work commitments and feel the need to do it all perfectly. We tend to feel responsible for everyone think we should be in control, and set ourselves ridiculously high standards.

Examples of over thinking include wondering over and over throughout the day, why you are suddenly feeling so old, or if your minor headaches could be a symptom of something more ominous and perhaps, even potentially deadly. It could mean lying awake at night thinking, "This economy is so bad, my investments are going to be worthless; I'm most certainly going to lose my job and I'll never be able to send my kids to college. "Or, it could mean thinking many times throughout the day about how unattractive your thinning and wispy hair was becoming. Gail Blanke, tell a story in her book "How to Stop Over thinking Your Life and Start Living", about being invited to the Financial Women's Association 2007 annual dinner, and how, knowing that she was going to meet and sit next to some very influential, and presumably, very well put together women, she became obsessed with picking the "right" outfit to wear. She discloses that she actually thought about it for days, and even made lists and sketches of all the alternatives, in her efforts to look perfect, until eventually, her daughter, who was 25 at the time said to her, "Why are you making this so hard? The invitation says, 'business attire.' Just wear the navy suit and have a good time." (She did and had a marvelous time.)

Other work related examples include, ruminating extensively about why your boss or colleague did not say something in support of the comments you made at an recent meeting. Dwelling on the situation and such thoughts as "Does that mean she thinks my ideas are stupid?", or, "Then again why has she not reacted to my email? It is been three days. Could he be angry about something? Is he punishing me? Am I just too unimportant to bother with?" can really get in the way of confidence, performance and productivity. Someone who spends enormous amounts of time wondering why a co-worker or superior hurrying down the hall did not make eye contact or speak to them, is setting themselves up for feeling badly, and subsequently, not feeling like it's worth it to put in the effort or take the risks involved for top performance.

Many people think that when they feel down, disappointed or discouraged by some events, that thinking about them extensively and analyzing the situation in order to figure it out will help. The reality, if we look at the science, is just the opposite. Rather than being helpful, endless ruminating about causes and explanations of possible negative events tends to make people feel worse. In fact, according to Lyubomirsky, there is vast and overwhelming evidence that thinking over and over (also called "rumination") about a disappointing or worrisome situation is bad for us. It can be so toxic, that it prevents us from taking important pro-active steps that could improve the situation and it can lead to an negative spiral toward an ever worsening mood, a negative distortion of reality, and even, in those who are vulnerable, clinical depression. Life, work and the world around us are full of problems, from minor annoyances, flaws and imperfections, to major tragedies and frightening risks and possibilities, but over thinking them does not make them better. Nor does it make us safer, or somehow less likely to be bothered or hurt by any of these vicissitudes. Instead, it makes us feel worse and makes us less likely to take positive action to improve our mood or actually change those situations which are changeable.

OVER THINKING YOUR LIFE

I have been thinking about lot lately about over-thinking. People like me who are a bit perfectionist and a bit obsessive are often guilty of it. In my case. I was set up for it by an family that made a production out of EVERYTHING from the contents of a dinner, to a day at the beach. If we went for an ice cream cone at Carvel, it was not a simple impulsive trip to the place three miles away, but a carefully constructed evening ride up the Taconic Parkway to the Carvel sixty miles north, complete with blankets and car games for the outing. Over thinking was reframed as creativity, diligence, thoroughness and spirit. Everything we did was elaborately planned, and for the most part we had great fun in the process.

Fast forward to the present. For the last twenty,(yes 20) years I have been thinking about hiring a billing service for my psychotherapy practice. The billing is the least favorite and most incompetent thing I have always done, struggling to keep up with the sheer volume of it daily.

I'm often apologetic about it to clients, or make jokes about my ineptness in that department. I rarely feel self doubt about the therapeutic work itself, just the damn billing. I have milled over the notion of relinquishing the control, the work involved in transferring the information to a service, the time it would take me, the cost, etc. This is what over thinking looks like when it is counterproductive, not artistic. So I have finally decided to let go of this the last vestige of self apology, and this exercise in over thinking I'm hiring a billing service! And what's the point of announcing this, you ask? To follow the Nike logo: JUST DO IT! Before getting caught in a spin of all the "how to" details, I will follow my own therapeutic advice and take one small step each day, breaking the task down into teeny weensy steps, and not think about it!

So if you too have an overactive brain that makes a production out of things, do four things to free yourself from the obsessive spin:

Ask yourself if you are over thinking an issue serves some larger creative, safety, or fun purpose, or not.

If not, decide what an reasonable person would do for action, without further ado.

Break the task or dilemma down into bite size pieces, day by day, and ignore your thoughts.

Build in time to "review" progress at intervals, not daily (that leads to more over thinking)

Then sit back and enjoy the completion without all the internal "noise"

How to overcome it?

If you are a chronic over thinker, simply being told to take time out and relax won't do it for you. You need to take active steps to control and overcome negative thinking. Breaking the habit isn't easy, and there's no magic solution for everyone, but these are some of the steps that experts suggest can help you break out of the negative cycle of over thinking.

Give yourself a break free your mind with something that engages your concentration and lifts your mood: whether it is reading a good book, walking the dog, having an massage or doing the gym.

Take yourself in hand: When you notice yourself going over the same thoughts, tell yourself firmly to stop. Post yellow stickers on your desk and around the house as reminders.

Ditch the delaying tactics: If there are particular situations or places that trigger over thinking, such as a desk piled high with papers or unanswered letters or emails, then do something about it, however small. Over thinking that's linked with inactivity can become a vicious cycle. Instead of living in fear of what you can't do and what could happen it's far better to tackle it simply by doing something.

Release your thoughts – Issues that assume mammoth proportions after frenetic worrying can suddenly melt away when you talk them throught with an friend. They can seem ridiculous or even funny. Making a joke out of them can really help to defuse your worries.

Schedule in thinking time – decide when you allow yourself to think. Limit the time you give yourself and stick to your schedule. Imagine keeping all those thoughts in a special box that you can take out at a particular time of the day, then seal and put it away when the time runs out.

Enjoy the moment – Actively plan things that you enjoy. It doesn't matter what it is – whatever works for you. It's hard to languish in negative over thinking when you're having fun.

Express your emotions – instead of going into a deep analysis of what your emotions really mean, just allow yourself to experience them for a change. Weep, scream, punch a pillow, allow yourself to feel the emotion and then move on.

Forgive yourself – That doesn't mean pretending that slight or hurtful remarks never happened but it does mean making a choice to put them aside rather than dwell on them.

Be mindful Take time each day just to be in the moment. It won' be easy, but persist and you will reap the rewards. Go out in the garden to watch the sunset. Spend 15 minutes in the park at lunchtime or sit in a café on your own. Don't banish the thoughts, let them come and go, but notice what's around and how your body feels.

OVER THINKING WILL CAUSE YOU TO THINK IT OVER

When was the last time you did something without actually spending a second to contemplate if it's the right thing to do? If you find it quite hard to make a decision even in the simplest things like deciding what to eat for breakfast, you may be a victim of what we call "over thinking".

A typical rational human being has a gift of reason which allows him to know the difference between good or bad. Sometimes, "reason" obliges us to think too much which causes us to be anxious in every decision we make. Finding hidden meaning in mere situations that does not require your investigative prowess worries your mind that you tend to become conscious in everything you do, constraining you from doing what you want. Over thinkers weigh each single option before they can make an move. They tend to ignore the bigger picture which causes them to panic under pressure even when they already know that they are good at it.

Growing up, we are filled with so much learning that we acquire so much knowledge which is good to a certain extent.

When you are not in the mood, you have the tendency to be anxious and get depressed. This will eventually trigger your mind to outpour thoughts. Sometimes, these thoughts are not even connected to the main reason why you are having a bad mood. When you start thinking too much, your normal functions are affected.

Stop seeing what is beyond the surface if there is no need to. Before you dig deeper, you must have a clear view of what is in front of you. If you continue to give weight to those that are unnecessary, you will fail to see the truth of everything.

When you start thinking about something in an endless cycle, ask yourself:

Will this still matter in the long run?

Asking yourself this simple question every time you over think can snap you out immediately. You will then be able to focus your time on something that really matters. Learn to set a time-limit for every decision you make so that you can immediately act on it. Be better in making decisions by setting "deadlines" in your life in order to prevent you from procrastinating and encourage you to not take things for granted.

Most of us wishes we could control everything that is happening. If this was only possible, we could have avoided making an mistake and things would have been perfect. But failures are a part of life and this is the only time where we can learn an lesson and become a better person. Everyone who is successful made mistakes before they reach their status quo.

Stop thinking over and over and over, it will just be an endless cycle and none of it matters. You can not control everything. Accept the fact there are just things that are beyond what you can handle.

There is no need to dwell on things that do not matter. Focus on what is important like making those people close to you smile. You can easily grab a bunch of alluring blossoms through flowers delivery.

Chapter 9: How Your Mind Works And

Why You Think The Way You Do

There is a strong connection between your mind and your brain and perhaps, this is the strongest connection that exists in you. Still, you would probably would give more credit to your brain for most of the things you do, even though those things may have been the work of your mind. While your brain is responsible for receiving signals from the other parts of your body, your mind is responsible for processing the results of these signals and further sending messages to your brain to put the right part of your body to work.

The thing is, while your brain is a key part of your existence, your mind is much stronger than you think. Have you thought of the greatest achievers and thinkers in the world? What is it that helped them achieve so much? Is it merely their brain, environment, and experiences or was there something else that contributed to all of these to help them succeed? In this section, we will be looking into the power of the mind, and the way it works. Certainly, there are a lot of limitations that can hinder your progress but all those limitations that you see are only physical, the mind is boundless and as such, there are no limitations for it; It is possible to have the mind of a Navy SEAL.

To get a full grasp of the abilities of the mind, you have to first understand the way it works. According to Caroline Ferguson, a mindset trainer at carolineferguson.com, the ability to manage the mind helps in understanding the things that go on in the brain. One does not have to be a brain surgeon or a neuroscientist before one can be curious about the functionalities of the brain. In an attempt to describe the mind, she first explains the connection between the brain and the mind. In her article about the way the mind works, she likens the brain to a computer. The brain is the hardware, which is the physical box that has all the power, the storage, wiring, processing power as well as the memory, which everyone needs to be able to function as a human being. The mind, on the other hand, is the software, which is the operating system that helps in gathering, storing and managing information by making use of the huge processing resources that are available in the brain. In a nutshell, the brain and the mind are integral parts of the same entity and they both cannot function without the other. They are simply inseparable.

Typically, thoughts are generated by the mind, which has several levels of consciousness.

The Conscious Mind

According to scientists, the conscious mind takes up about 10% of the total operational power of the mind and is what is responsible for the following:

- Gathering of data

- Processing and assessing data that has been collected
- Looking for patterns and comparing them
- Giving orders and making decisions
- Gives you the ability to give a thoughtful response to situations instead of responding in an insensitive way
- Having control of short-term memories

When you are considering things in your conscious mind, those things are deliberate, such that you are very aware of them.

The Unconscious Mind

90% of the things that takes place in the mind happen thanks to the unconscious mind. You may not always be aware of the things that happens in this part of the mind as a result of the fact that you are always not aware of the things that happen here, but the truth is that the unconscious mind has a lot of power. Here are some of its strengths:

• It is responsible for major workings of the body like sleeping, temperature control, digestion, breathing, heart rate, sleeping and so on. All these happen without your knowledge or conscious effort/contribution and it is the conscious mind that controls this phenomenon.

• Find shield or protection for you by helping you to stick to the status quo. It is for this reason that you always seem somehow uncomfortable whenever you consider making a change. When there seems to be a possible change in sight, the mind takes you back to what it considers to be familiar and/or safe.

• It houses all of your emotions.

• It is the powerhouse of every form of creativity and imagination that you exhibit.

• The mind creates and maintains your habits.

• It takes and obeys instructions from the conscious mind.

• When there is a threat from the outside (or even internal threats like ill health), the unconscious mind makes you react automatically. In the face of threats, the mind may tell you to either run, freeze, or fight back as a response.

● The unconscious mind houses, stores, and retrieve long-term memories.

Generally, the unconscious mind isn't rational, as it does not send signals to you for logic and reason before taking action. It does not operate with judgment and it typically cannot distinguish between what is right and what is wrong as well as what is good or bad. What it does is to simply accept the things that it is told or given as the truth and this is regardless of how true the information is. The way you think, feel, and behave is, however, in line with the consistency of the information that the unconscious mind receives.

The Importance of Knowing How the Mind Works

As an individual and as a human, there is a need for you to understand the way the mind works because this knowledge enables you to use the combined strength of both the conscious and the unconscious mind in order to think in a much more healthy, resilient, flexible, and goal-supporting manner.

If you can master the way your mind works, your self-worth will be improved such that you will have much less emotional upheaval and a higher chance of achieving the things that you want in life.

The unconscious mind also helps in the formation and the maintenance of habits, whether good or bad.

Why You Think the Way You Do

Generally, your success in life is largely dependent on the things that happen in your life and the way you perceive them. While your environment plays a large role in the way behave and think, there is more to it than just your environment. Chances are, if you were subjected to the same conditions as another person, your reactions to things would still be different.

This is because regardless of the environment, the nature of humans is dynamic. While you may react negatively to some things, another person may positively react to them.

Considering that the mind is responsible for our thoughts, it is first important to note that the mind does not work independently regardless of whether it is the conscious or the unconscious mind. As explained in the earlier part of this chapter, the conscious mind takes cues from the brain as well as the environment to act. These cues are as a result of our experiences, as well as the influence of our immediate environment. This will help us to gather and process data, make decisions, give responses in a thoughtful manner as well as control our short-term memory. There is also the influence of our biological make-up in the way we think and this is part of what happens in the unconscious mind. The environment and experiences of a person also contribute to this aspect.

Have you ever wondered why some people tend to be more reactive than others? This is regardless of whether they have been through certain harsh conditions or not. Now here is the difference between the role of the environment and the nature of the person. Let's take two people who have lived in a troubled environment for example. Because there have been crises in their immediate environment, they have both experienced a lot of gunshots and deaths amidst other harsh conditions. When they are taken out of this environment, they are expected to become more relaxed. What then happens if, in their relaxed state, there is the sound of a gunshot? Chances are that while person A may panic and think of taking a flight to avoid imminent danger, person B may not be that reactive because he may have told himself that he has been through worse where he has come from. While their reactions are both born out of their experiences, the outcome of it, which is either fear or boldness, comes from their nature. This is the reason why siblings who were raised under the same conditions may not necessarily have the same character. While one may be more strong-willed, the other may be more cowardly. Psychologists describe this phenomenon as the role of nature and nurture in the cognitive development of a person.

While some psychologists believe that nature plays a bigger role in cognitive development, others believe that nurture plays a bigger role in the cognitive development of a person. When one thinks of the mind of a person and the way it works, it seems valid to say that nature and nurture interact to determine the way people think and react to things.

Chapter 10: What In The World Is Going On?

I was so sure of the future. It was a year when things were starting to come together for our family: my son was accepted at the same private school that I was teaching math, and my husband's business was finally picking up. We had recently built a new house. Life was beautiful and I felt completely blessed. I loved being a teacher and thought I would be doing it beyond retirement. And then...bam! My life spiraled down, fast.

I remember one day in particular. I had just left the house to go to work when I realized my car had a flat tire. Thankfully the mechanic was passing by and was kind enough to help me with the spare tire. As I was calling in late, I'd become frustrated and stressed. When I got to school, I taught a couple of classes but was feeling off. I experienced tightness in my chest and had heart palpitations. When my left hand began feeling numb, I decided to have my heart checked. I often do things in an unconventional way. I didn't want to go to an emergency room and wait there for hours. Instead, I marched to the nearest cardiologist office during my lunch break. Having no appointment, I told the receptionist that I wanted to be seen. Thankfully, the doctor agreed and after he checked my heart and vital signs, became alarmed and called an ambulance to transport me to the ER. Even though the ER was so close that it shared a parking lot with the cardiologist's office, the doctor was taking no chances of sending me there alone. His office called for an ambulance and within minutes I was attended to by a group of paramedics. They put me on a stretcher and escorted me the whole ten minutes to a building next door. I was scared and thought I might have had a heart attack. The experience was very frightening and surreal. With a history of my father and his father both dying from heart attacks, I was extremely concerned.

A series of tests revealed that I was in no immediate danger. In a few hours I was released to go home. I had to see a cardiologist the following day because of a heart abnormality. After a few hours of additional tests the next day, the doctor told me I had to be admitted to a hospital for an emergency angiogram. I remember bursting into tears as I described to this doctor the events of the past couple of weeks. I became hysterical and was sobbing non-stop, remembering a parent-teacher conference that took place about ten days earlier. It didn't make sense at all. The event seemed rather ordinary. Why did this particular episode affect me so deeply? I've been through difficult situations in my life, some of which seemed much tougher than this. In the past I experienced loss, abuse, betrayal. I was totally bewildered by my extreme reaction. That is when I began recognizing a disconnection between my body's reactions and my thought process, realizing that this situation shouldn't have affected me so dramatically. Why in the world had I begun trembling and hyperventilating uncontrollably whenever I thought of facing a classroom again? I could **not** figure it out. That's the deal with panic attacks. They rarely make much sense. They randomly take over your whole being. I learned that it is the fight-or-flight response of the body to what it perceives as danger.

After the angiogram, I stayed at the hospital for a few days to be monitored. Doctors found a heart abnormality called Mitral Valve Prolapse. I learned not from doctors but from personal research that people with this heart condition are prone to anxiety and it is more common in women. Later, I also studied the subject of panic disorder.

Within days I realized I couldn't go back to work without feeling anxious and so had to take a leave of absence. Even at home, I had eight to ten panic attacks a day, each lasting over half an hour. Eventually I had to go on disability, as my condition was not improving fast enough. During the first months since being diagnosed, even driving by the school building threw me into a full-blown panic attack. When I had to go back to collect my belongings, I had to hang onto my friend, holding her hand tight. I thought if I didn't do that, I would collapse. I was literally trembling and feeling dizzy.

I had revealing conversations with my doctor and psychologist about why I wasn't able to teach. Part of it was a fear of going into hyperventilation in the middle of a lesson and frightening my students. There were other layers of fears and concerns I discovered in therapy sessions, in conversations with doctors and by studying the subject of anxiety and mental health. My body was responding to various triggers I was not able to recognize at that time. My physical responses didn't make any sense to me.

At first I didn't think a cure was possible. I thought I was going to die; the pain was so intense each time that I was afraid for my life. Knowing that my father died at the age of forty-six from a heart attack may have exacerbated the situation. My poor husband and son bore the greatest burden, seeing me catapulted into a dark emotional and physical place without warning.

A while later, I recalled a few events when I experienced similar symptoms on a much smaller scale. The first time it happened, I was still living in Ukraine. On a particularly hot day, I was huffing and puffing up the hill to get to my place of work and felt tightness in my chest and shortness of breath. I got a bit concerned, but not much. I thought it was just the heat getting to me and didn't go to see a doctor right away. This occurred around the time when things got tense at work: the principal of the school I was working at the time was very unfair with teachers. He acted like a tyrant and it bothered me deeply. The principal was the only male treating all the female staff as if he owned the place. When he brought one of my colleagues to tears over something miniscule, I became upset. I'm always for the underdog and a big desire is for people to get along. Later on I was looking for behavior patterns in my life that led to anxiety. Witnessing unfairness to others is one thing that affects me deeply.

I was back to normal in a few days, tightness in my chest dissipated and I didn't think about this episode until much later.

The second time it happened I had started teaching at a school here in California. The teacher with whom I was sharing a classroom may not have liked me being there. How did I guess? She made a habit of cooking her lunch in our shared classroom in a toaster oven in the middle of my geometry class. I understood she wanted to eat healthy meals and prepare them fresh, but really! I hated confrontation of any sort so I politely asked a few times for her to stop, which she ignored. I had to resolve it somehow, so I complained to my supervisor, to no avail. After a month of these "Geometry Cooking Classes," I dreaded coming to work.

Now that I look back, it doesn't surprise me that eventually I became very stressed. As a result, one not so beautiful morning, I had to be rushed to an ER because I thought I was having a heart attack. The symptoms were similar: shortness of breath, tension in the neck and shoulders, numbness in my left arm down to my fingers, as well as chest pain. Pesky panic attacks mimic heart attacks but thankfully, only in symptoms. In anxiety attacks, the heart is not at risk, even if it feels very much at risk. After a complete checkup, I was released without a diagnosis, and my heart was okay. What a relief! Still, I remember feeling extremely guilty, as nothing was seriously wrong with my health. I alarmed my colleagues and missed a day of work for nothing! Many women feel guilty for bothering others unless they are dying. I will share more about such stoicism and guilt later.

Beginning of the Healing Journey

It was nobody's fault. It was the way my body perceived a stressful situation and reacted to seeming threat. This is what happens during anxiety and panic attacks: a natural body response to perceived danger, also called fight or flight reaction. Muscles involuntarily tense up, breathing and heartbeat become rapid and we become basically paralyzed with fear, like a rabbit in front of a rattlesnake.

It took time to realize that my illness was not going to destroy me

School administrators and colleagues at my work were concerned. As time passed a few confided in me that they had panic attacks too. I was corresponding via email with the headmaster, with whom I also had a meeting. These conversations contributed to the creation of a school-wide tutoring program that was quite overdue and was launched shortly after. It was the first positive result from a lot of negativity. It helped to look for meaning in life's most unfortunate events and to switch to a positive perspective.

It took time to realize that my illness was not going to destroy me. This challenge in life, like so many others, was to teach and improve me even though in the beginning it was nearly impossible to see any positive aspect of this extremely painful experience. It took a long time but now I can look back with gratitude, appreciating the lessons learned. My hope for all of us is to become better, not bitter as we go through life's inevitable challenges.

At first none of what I was experiencing made any sense at all. I was a total mess, surrounded by almost palpable darkness.

Ever so slowly it began to get lighter and lighter. Eventually I saw my situation as a dark tunnel with light shining at the end of it. Finally the day came when a bright light was shining in my life again. My senses returned, I could see, feel, smell and experience joy once again. I was back!

A little over two years—that is how long it took me to overcome severe debilitating panic attacks and get my life back on track. Overcoming mild anxiety relapses took much longer, but those subsided as well. Trust me, it was not easy, but healing proved to be possible. I emerged on the other side stronger, more equipped to face life's inevitable challenges and detours. I became passionate about helping others. Now I look forward to sharing what I have learned along the way with those who seek release from the grip of stress and anxiety.

Chapter 11: Negative Emotions

According to Pam (2013), Negative emotion can be defined as unpleasant or unhappy emotions that were triggered in an individual to express a negative effect, particularly towards a situation or another individual.

Here are a few basic emotions:

Anger

Disgust

Fear

Happiness

Sadness

Surprise

Additional emotions (later included as part of a more expansive view of emotion) were included by renowned psychologist Eckman:

Amusement

Contempt

Contentment

Embarrassment

Guilt

Pride
Relief
Satisfaction
Sensory pleasure
Shame

With this list of emotions, we can vividly see which emotions have been deemed negative, such as Guilt, Shame, Embarrassment, etc. However, it is not the negative emotions that affect our well-being; rather, it is the ways and manner in which we react to them that affects us and also helps to determine our health status.

Being stuck in negative emotions would increase one's body's production of worry hormones and cortisol. With this, the cognitive ability to solve a problem, and to be proactive, is depleted. Also, it can damage our immune system by making it susceptible to other forms of illness. It is important to note that chronic worry has been revealed to be linked to a shorter life span.

In another sphere of study, the researcher has begun to look into what could be the link between negative emotions and cancer. While delving in, researchers based their focus on anger as a negative emotion and its link to cancer. It was mentioned earlier that negative emotion has positive effects, but an individual's reaction to their emotions is what will make it them better or worse. Anger is a normal feeling, but whether it is healthy depends on how it being expressed or not expressed. It's the manner of this expression that may sometimes cause problems. Anger could be referred to as unhealthy anger when it is intense, prolonged, or repressed. Unhealthy anger has been linked to cancer. However, another study revealed that patients with cancer presented an extremely low score of anger in a tested environment, and they suggested that the patients were either repressing or suppressing their anger. Researchers then suggested that anger could be a precursor to the development of cancer.

Further evidence supports the claim about the link between anger and cancer. One statistic showed the positive relationship between the extreme repression of anger and breast cancer diagnoses. According to research, women repressing their anger showed an increase in levels of the serum Immunoglobulin A, and this has been linked to some autoimmune diseases.

IN WHAT CAPACITY CAN WE CONTROL OUR NEGATIVE EMOTIONS?

The possible best way of dealing with negative emotions is through acceptance. As there are benefits to negative emotions, compelling ourselves to be happy most of the time can similarly be ominous to our well-being.

Enduring adverse emotion in ourselves, and other individuals, empowers us to develop sympathy for how they may present themselves and empathy for why they may present themselves. Rather than getting stuck in a viewpoint that negative emotions ought to be avoided or that they are somehow 'wrong' to experience, we need to recognize they are essential elements of our character.

When we do that, we can genuinely begin to change how we may respond to them and create practices that are meaningful and help us to engage more positively with others.

Chapter 12: What Is Overthinking And

What Are The Causes?

There are various situations in our lives when we keep on thinking about a certain thing all day long. You might think that it is completely normal when you keep on having thoughts about something, such as any situation, behavior, or even thinking about a performance that you will have to do after a few days. But, in actual, it is not. When you are thinking too much about something, you are actually overthinking.

Many people think that when you overthink, you are most likely suffering from overthinking disorder. But, in actuality, there is nothing like an overthinking disorder. There are various types of disorders that come along with anxiety when an individual engages himself/herself in rumination or overthinking, but that is not a disorder. When you cannot stop obsessing and worry over things, it can actually interfere with your life quality. You might be wondering that what actually is overthinking. Some of the psychological diagnoses that have been done in which an individual cannot actually stop their brain from overthinking are actually the signs of trauma, PTSD, panic disorder, separation anxiety disorder, agoraphobia, social anxiety disorder, or it could be the signs of some other form of illness.

When it comes to the topic of overthinking, you might even think of it as a symptom. For instance, an individual who suffers from panic disorder might also ruminate and keep on thinking when he/she is going to experience an attack of panic again. Such individuals are most likely to obsess over anything which could actually trigger the attack. They are not only suffering from anxiety now, but they are having now meta-anxiety as well, which is nothing but getting anxiety about becoming anxious again. Overthinking is very common. You are not required to have an anxiety disorder for engaging yourself in continuous rumination. You can say it is a part of the condition of human beings. All human beings overthink at certain points in their life. You might become very conscious about what you said or did to someone close to you, or you might also become worried about some performance at work or at any function. These are the examples when are most likely to get engaged with overthinking.

Some other examples of overthinking are:

Worrying about how to measure up to the other individuals at work.

Obsessing about what you should have done or said.

Thinking about the worst scenarios.

Obsessive kind of thoughts.

Engaging yourself in 'what-if' situations.

Overthinking is actually pervasive in nature. But, it also comes along with required help for such conditions. There are many people around us who worry and obsess about such things that are out of their hands or control in reality. The most common form of treatment for this type of condition is CBT or Cognitive Behavior Therapy. CBT helps the sufferers to challenge their irrational or negative thinking, which ultimately helps in changing their thoughts into taking positive and productive shape. Let's learn about overthinking detail first.

Overthinking

Most of you are familiar with the famous term 'anxiety disorder.' But, in most of the cases, people tend to overlook one certain symptom of anxiety disorder, which is overthinking. The primary definition of overthinking is to obsess or ruminate about something. Many people, while coming across this definition, might think of themselves as being overthinkers. Who actually does not think twice about something in their daily lives? Human beings have the nature of wondering about making the perfect choice from very small things like choosing the easiest route for the commute to choosing the correct restaurant for a dinner night or thinking about the safety and security of your family. It is very much normal. It is really a common thing to worry and also to overthink up to a certain extent.

But, overthinking does come with certain harmful effects that can impact on your emotional as well as mental health. When overthinking pertains to anxiety disorder, it is most likely to have excessive, overwhelming thoughts about anything which leads to stress, anxiety, fear, or even dread. It is not only about thinking excessively about something, but it is also actually having an obsession with something so much that it will be ultimately affecting the functioning of your life. When you start wondering or worrying about your life, friends, family or something else and if you do not have the issue of overthinking, whatever you are thinking about will be worrying you only for some time, and then after a certain point of time, you will be going on with your normal day. You worry at times but are not ruminating continuously. You are not finding that the worry is actually interfering with your everyday life. This is normal.

With overthinking as the ultimate result of anxiety disorder, the concerned person can always think about, and even they might not be obsessing on the same kind of thing every time, they actually remain concerned regarding something all the time. If you think that you are suffering from overthinking due to anxiety disorder, you might find that you must have experienced any of these situations:

Having difficulty in going along or contributing to any conversation as you are most likely to go over the potential form of statements or responses or the opportunity to actually speak up has been lost.

Continuously measuring your very own self with others and trying to figure out how you measure to them.

Reliving all your past form of failures and mistakes all over again from time to time, and you cannot move away from your past.

Focusing on the scenarios of worst-case.

Reliving any past experience of trauma.

Unable to slow down the pace of racing thoughts, emotions, and worries.

It is very unlikely to find out that two people are experiencing overthinking in the exact same way. Those who experience overthinking will find out that the ultimate quality of their life is being compromised because of the inability to control all of their negative thoughts along with emotions. It might make it difficult for you to move out and mix with other people or socialize, enjoy your hobbies, try to be productive at your work as your mind is most likely to spend a considerable portion of time along with your energy in thinking about particular thought lines. In severe cases, it might also become very tough to control your mind along with your emotions, and this might turn out to be very damaging for your own mental health.

It might turn out to be very difficult for you to make new friends or even to keep up with your already existing friends as you are most likely to struggle in communicating if anything goes wrong or might turn out to be communicating more than required. It can also be very tough for you to speak up as you are overly concerned about how you will be doing it right or what will be happening next. An individual who suffers from overthinking might even find it very difficult to continue with a general form of conversation or to interact normally in a casual environment.

The truth behind this is, overthinking can actually affect almost everything and anything in your life. It can affect the whole way in which you love to work with others, impact your very own social life, and will also be taking a toll on your very own personal life. In simple words, it can begin to wear away all your relationships with the people all around you.

Causes of overthinking

If you are suffering from overthinking, you must have come thought about the question, what is the reason behind it? Why does it sound like an illness? Such questions are most likely to keep on coming. However, in most of the cases, the causes are overthinking are definite in nature. The most common causes are:

Caring: You are most likely to suffer from overthinking if you care about certain people in your life. In such cases, you are most likely think of doing things that will be loved by your close ones, and at the same time, you are most likely to think that what they would think if anything goes wrong or something else takes place.

Lack of confidence: You must have come across the saying that confidence is the key to success. It is something that can drive you to the top. When you lack it, you start overthinking. It is mostly because you cannot trust yourself and start doubting yourself after doing something. What this results in is overthinking along with under-performing what you do the best. Overthinking triggered by a lack of confidence might turn out to be deadly for your mental health as you will find it difficult to properly do anything or even decide to do anything just because of the fear that you will not be able to do the things right.

Thinking yourself of being at fault: When you start thinking of yourself of being the center of everything and also think you are the one who is at fault, you are most likely to experience overthinking. In such situations, you will always be finding yourself at fault and start to think awkward situations that won't happen ever. It will also be stopping you from taking part in things that you love, and you are most likely to find it difficult to socialize with people around you.

Past trauma or incidents: Overthinking can also crop up due to any past incident which you cannot actually forget or erase from your mind. It can be an incident of extreme sorrow or an event of great humiliation where you were ashamed of doing something wrong.

Human beings overthink as we are desperate living beings who are always hunting for some answers. Human beings love certainty and also love to be in control. Not to be worried as it is also a part of the survival tactic of humans. Overthinking is nothing but 90% of fear of 10% of unwanted thoughts. Human beings cannot predict the future, and that is why we are most likely to overthink certain situations like what will happen if we do this or what will be the reaction of others? Will I be able to pull off the performance properly? This ultimately results in ruining the actual scenario, and you are most likely to end up underperforming.

The intuition of human beings gives out half of the ability to do that. Human beings come along with a very powerful voice inside, which actually helps in saving us in various situations, but at times, it might also dysfunction just because of overthinking. So, it is necessary to cope up with overthinking to get the best from our lives.

Overthinking is coupled, along with fear. Fear acts like the seed of a treacherous form of a tree. Human beings are not born along with fear; it adapts with the imparted life lessons along with traumas and life experiences. Human beings have very little or almost no control over what was done or taught to us in our childhood. The majority of the people who are suffering from overthinking are actually living with the branches of fear inside them from which they are developing their extra thoughts. Various things happen with us in our relationships, childhood, jobs, and friendships, and the worst part of those experiences are most likely to latch with the rest of our lives.

The past experiences and thoughts surface like the settled form of poison, which oozes through the human brain in the moments of overthinking. You are responsible for creating such patterns of thought. You keep on thinking about what happened with you in the past, and the ugly part of such experiences is most likely to trigger overthinking. You need to remember that the more you think, the more amount of fear you will be inviting in your life. Overthinking can have adverse effects on human lives, and it can alter the normal styles of living. If you think that you are suffering from overthinking, follow the tips in the following chapters for getting away from it.

Chapter 13: What Is Overthinking?

There are two facets to overthinking; the first is ruminating (going over and over the same things) about the past and the second is worrying about the future.

Of course, it is natural for us to worry at some time or another. For example, imagine you have an interview booked. You may worry about getting there on time, you may worry about not being able to answer a question. This may lead you to checking a route and planning to set off earlier to make sure you are there on time. It may lead you to prepare, maybe even practice answering questions to yourself in the mirror or looking online to see what common interview questions there are and then trying to answer them based on your own experience and knowledge. In this scenario, planning a route and practicing your answers is not only sensible, but productive, as you know you will attend that interview and be prepared.

For some people faced with a situation like this however their minds goes into overdrive. They may start to panic and imagine the worst possible scenarios over and over such as being stuck in traffic or missing their bus and being late, becoming flustered and not being able to speak or their mind going blank so they can't answer any questions. They may look up the route and how long it takes to get there several times a day. They may start to ask themselves "what if" questions such as "What if they don't like me?", "What if there are people with more experience than me?", "What if I get lost?", "What if I don't know the answer to anything and they think I'm stupid?" They go over and over these same questions and negative scenarios to the point that rather than doing something constructive to prepare, they are simply worrying.

Why Do We Overthink?

As humans we are constantly trying to make sense of the world around us. We want to be in control yet there are some things we can't control such as the weather, other people's actions or emotions or the future. We still try to predict outcomes however and this is when we can get into a cycle of overthinking. Another reason for overthinking is that we strive for perfection. We want to be the best we can possibly be but this can lead to us worrying that we maybe aren't as good as we think we are.

Why Is Overthinking Bad?

Overthinking stems from fear. This fear plants a seed of doubt into our minds, which we struggle to ignore. Once we start to doubt ourselves it becomes difficult to make decisions and trust our instincts.

There is nothing wrong with worrying and thinking problems through or trying to plan for the future to a certain extent but overthinking is an issue if it becomes debilitating enough that it prevents us from achieving anything. Sometimes we find ourselves in a situation where we are so paralyzed with fear that we just freeze. We don't do what we should do because we are frightened it won't be as perfect as we want it to be.

Relationships can be affected. We may talk to family and friends looking for clarification on a situation but not finding comfort in their reassurances, we may repeat ourselves over and over which can in turn start to alienate them. Something as innocuous as a conversation with a friend may be replayed over and over until it takes on a sinister feel. Are they really saying what we thought they were saying or did they mean something else? Were your friends just joking when they teased you about something you did or are they really talking about you behind your back? Suddenly we start to doubt ourselves and don't know who to trust. This in turn leads to us not wanting to make a decision in case we get it wrong which to other people makes it appear like we don't have an opinion about anything.

Overthinking can lead to a destructive thought process not only because going over and over the same things is exhausting but also because it isn't productive. You cannot change the past nor do you have full control over the future. Let's be honest, nobody ever overthinks anything positive and all these negative thoughts have a detrimental effect on our wellbeing. Once we begin on a destructive thought pattern it becomes increasingly difficult to get out of it.

Whilst overthinking in itself is not a recognized disorder yet it is linked to many mental health problems such as depression, OCD (Obsessive Compulsive Disorder) and, of course, anxiety. Someone who is an over-thinker can end up in a Catch-22 type situation; they start to overthink and worry and this in turn makes their mental health decline and they start to feel low or have high levels of anxiety which then makes them overthink and worry more and so it goes on.

Chapter 14: How To De-Clutter Your Mind

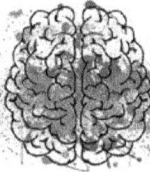

The vast majority of us have a mind brimming with clutter. There is something more terrible than having a cluttered home or workspace, and that is having a cluttered personality. A cluttered personality is anxious and unfocused. It attempts to move in a wide range of bearings immediately and the outcome is quite negative.

Mental clutter can incorporate the majority of the following: agonizing over the future; ruminating about the past, keeping a psychological plan for the day and grumblings. Luckily, there are methodologies and strategies you can use to wipe out some space in your mind.

Beneath you will discover the different ways to de-clutter your mind so you can quit feeling so overwhelmed, accomplish more, and get greater clearness.

1. Record It.

You do not have to keep everything put away in your mind. Pick an apparatus—it very well may be an online instrument, an application, or even a stack of paper—and consider it a capacity gadget for each one of those odds and ends of information that you have to recall. This can incorporate arrangements, telephone numbers and thoughts for future ventures.

2. Figure out how to Meditate.

Fundamentally, contemplation is figuring out how to concentrate the brain totally on the present minute. When you figure out how to put the majority of your consideration on a certain something, for example, your breath– every single other idea vanish. It is nearly what could be compared to taking your brain through a vehicle wash and having futile and pointless musings washed away.

3. Keep a Journal.

Keeping a diary is like the last point, record it yet with more profundity. A diary enables you to download the inward prattle that is always interfering with your point of view when you are attempting to complete significant things. For instance, you can write in your diary about the accompanying things that you are stressed over; plans for accomplishing a significant objective or even worry about a relationship that is depleting your vitality.

4. Be Decisive.

On the off chance that your inbox is loaded up with reports, however, you neglect to settle on choices on how to manage everyone, what will occur? Before long, your inbox will overflow with letters, charges, and demands from imminent customers. The best approach to clear your inbox is by settling on a choice about how to manage each bit of paper that is in there.

Something very similar applies to your cerebrum. In the event that you put off deciding, your mind will, before long, be overflowing with the majority of the choices that you have to make. The arrangement is to be unequivocal.

For straightforward choices, pursue a methodology. When you have to settle on progressively significant and complex choices, apply an increasingly intensive methodology to help you

5. Relinquish the Past.

Mind clutter is regularly identified with the past. A great many people keep an enormous bureau of mental drawers put away in the back of their minds. These drawers are loaded up with slip-ups they have made, open doors they have missed, individuals they have harmed and past complaints.

Set aside the effort to experience those psychological drawers and dispose of recollections of the past that are not serving you well and are simply cluttering up your present life.

6. De-clutter Your Physical Environment.

Physical clutter prompts mental clutter. Above all else, clutter shells the brain with exorbitant improvements, which powers the mind to stay at work longer than required. Also, physical clutter sign to the mind that there is continually something different that should be done, which is rationally debilitating. As you de-clutter your physical space you'll discover that your brain is likewise de-cluttered.

7. Stop Multi-Tasking.

On the off chance that your home is a wreck and you have to arrange and de-clutter it, how might you start? You would most likely begin by picking one significant territory—for instance, the kitchen table—and clearing it of all clutter.

What could be compared to tidying up the kitchen table is to pick a specific measure of time which you will commit solely to one significant undertaking. During that time push all psychological clutter to the side and spotlight the majority of your consideration on the job needing to be done.

Picture a table that is clear everything being equal, with the exception of the one undertaking which you will take a shot at. Ensure that the table avoids every single other thing during the whole piece of time that you have committed to this assignment. On the off chance that whatever else attempts to work its direction onto the table, drive it off.

8. Organize.

Nothing makes as much mind clutter as an unending daily agenda. Acknowledge that you cannot do everything, and center on the things which are most essential to you. Make a short rundown of your top needs, and ensure that the main part of your mind space is committed to the things on that rundown.

9. Put Routine Decisions on Auto-Pilot.

Little, routine undertakings can involve a great deal of cerebrum space. This can incorporate things, for example, the accompanying:

Choosing what you are going to wear every day;

Choosing what to have for breakfast every day you wake up;

Settling on a choice on what to have for your main meal.

You can diminish the measure of brain space that is taken up by these normal errands by putting them on auto-pilot.

10. The Amount of Information You Receive Should Be Limited.

An excessive amount of information can stop up the cerebrum. This incorporates the information that you take in every day by perusing papers, online journals, and magazines; staring at the television screen; taking an interest in internet-based life; surfing the web on your advanced mobile phone, etc.

Limit the measure of information that comes into your life—and make space in your cerebrum by doing the accompanying:

Set a limit on the measure of time that you will spend via web-based networking media locales or perusing the web. Withdraw from any online journals and drop any magazine memberships that are not adding to your personal satisfaction or your prosperity. Ensure that the sentiments that you focus on originate from well-respected people with pertinent qualifications. Choose the information that is significant to you and neglect everything else.

Chapter 15: Foods For The Brain

If you want to increase brain power and maximize memory, the consumption of nutritious foods is very helpful. So, what are the best foods for the brain? It's too simple to single out our particular food (or foods) as being "best" for memory.

Since remembering engages a good bit of brain action, and brain activity puts special importance on a healthy nervous system and healthy blood flow, all steps you can take to improve your blood flow, circulation, and nervous system purpose may end up contributing to better memory.

Breakfast is the vital system of food because our health is confronted with various physical and mental activities and to neutralize the consequence, the proper awareness towards breakfast and other food habits is inevitable and intake must fulfill the required caloric value. A fueling breakfast helps us to incite high energy levels with a pouring effect on memory power.

Further, food ingestion must focus on well-adjusted calories, fueling and more importantly, a low-fat breakfast. Memory power is encouraged by the consumption and nourishing of a precise calorie breakfast. The learning system depends on memory power. If you possess high memory power, your learning curve will undoubtedly increase.

Some vegetables are rich in antioxidants, and antioxidants could perhaps help memory with the removal of harmful free radicals. The ones that might help are purple fruits and green leafy vegetables such as kale and spinach, and non-leafy greens such as broccoli.

We do not know where you live and therefore which fruits and vegetables you have available so we would just say that it would be good to look for ones that are deep in color... such as deep green (like leafy greens such as mustard greens, kale, broccoli, etc.), Deep orange (papaya, sweet potato, winter squash, etc.), Dark blue (berries, eggplant, purple cabbage, etc.) And deep red (berries, cherries, tomatoes, peppers, etc.).

What you do in your life can have an effect on your memory. If you make no effort to maintain or improve your memory, it will fail. Excessive drinking and smoking have direct and long-term negative effects on your memory so get away from them if you can. These bad habits will damage your gray matter.

Unhealthy eating habits and the quality of the food you eat will also affect the efficiency of your brain. An awful lot is written on this topic that it merely needs to be stated that a strong brain feeds from a healthy eating plan.

Emotional stress weakens the entire body and the immune system. It also damages your mental processes. It is difficult to keep away from stress these days, so it is very important to find ways to relax and to sleep well every day. Consider as a minimum some gentle exercising if you usually do not do so already and meditating. It makes your brain power of good.

You are what you eat which, determines who you are. If you want to increase your brain power, you should make sure that you include in your diet what is often called brain food. This is food that contains choline and proteins which help in the growth of the brain.

Fish such as tuna and salmon are considered particularly beneficial for your gray matter. Other brain foods include white meats, soya, tofu, milk and peanuts, which are fruit and vegetables in proteins. Fresh fruit and vegetables can also help by keeping the body strong and healthy. Youngsters definitely should be encouraged to eat plenty of these foods.

TRAIN THE BRAIN

Most people have a difficult time committing to a regimen of daily meditation. We live in a society where accomplishments are equated with hard work, pains, and struggle. Meditation is the exact opposite as it is about stillness and clearing of the mind. The accomplishment remains but in an entirely different area. One achieves a true sense of power through learning how to turn off the noise in their minds. The result is a much calmer, less reactive mind, leading to a far less reactive body. Decision making improves as a cooler head prevails. Life becomes easier due to a few short moments out of your schedule.

There are options and more palatable approaches concerning meditation, beyond the traditional twenty minutes, twice a day, for those who are locked into tight schedules. Traditional approaches have given way to more time effective methods that are simple to use, highly effective, and fit into one's daily routine, with benefits that continue to add to one's quality of life.

The New Approach to Meditation:

(1) The 5 Minute Meditation-

Most would be willing to relinquish five short minutes of their day to a routine that offers noticeable benefits from both their physical and emotional health, especially if one of the benefits was becoming less reactive to stress and tension. Dan Harris, news anchor and author, mentions this in his book "10% Happier" where he shares his own compelling story about his struggle with anxiety and how meditation dramatically changed his life. Through learning how to use mediation, even at five-minute intervals, he experienced a true affinity for this form of therapy and believes it can induce the same benefits for anyone on the go who still seeks the peace of mind in the shortest decompression time.

The concept, as described by Dan, is to maintain a straight spine, preferably sitting in a chair, close your eyes and become consciously aware of your breath (where you feel it the most: nose, chest, belly) Focus on how this breath feels as you inhale and exhale. Every time your mind begins to wander (which it always does), gently yet firmly guide it back to the breath.

This short exercise is beneficial in more ways than one can imagine and is addictive in nature. Feeling well, composed and in charge of yourself is the catalyst for continuation.

(2) Meditation Through Activity/Exercise

As children, we went outdoors to play and make no mistake, that's exactly what we did, PLAY. Nowadays, one takes a short break from their daily routine and desperately tries to reap the benefits of exercise. Unfortunately, they feel no better emotionally after the initial "pump" wears off. This is because they are also bringing along an additional friend to their exercise routine. This friend is their "overactive mind."

They had planned to use this time to relax, let off steam, and enjoy the great outdoors: but end up unfocused, thinking about past worries, future events, current agitations and anything but the peace and serenity they seek in the present moment of what should be a relaxing exercise routine.

The answer is clear. Learn to turn your mind off while using an exercise routine at the same time. This is doable while walking, running, swimming or any other type of activity that involves movement, preferably outdoors and alone. Here are the steps:

Focus on your breath as you walk.

Become consciously aware of the repetition of your footsteps or body movement.

Use your senses: sight, sound, smell as you breathe in the air.

When intrusive thoughts slip in, gently but firmly sweep them aside and go back to focusing on your breath and/or body movement.

Enjoy the moment without dragging in thoughts about past events or future ones that have yet to occur. Be the child again who loses him or herself in the activity. This is childlike, not childish.

(3) Meditation as a Sleep Enhancer

Many people occasionally find difficulty in falling asleep at night. They toss and turn and become agitated when the hours pass without restful sleep. They become cranky the next day and experience a true lack of productivity, not to mention a diminished sense of well being. They take their work, worries, fears, anger, and grudges to bed with them at night. This is a definite sleep blocker and requires a bit of discipline to overcome, but it's simple to follow and produces fantastic results. Just follow the steps:

Make sure your bedroom is cool in temperature by cracking a window and allowing fresh air to enter the room. This enhances sleep and refreshes the body.

Lie on your back and keep your spine straight. Make sure your bedclothes are loose and arms by your side, rather than crossed upon your body.

Become consciously aware of your breath as you inhale through your nose and follow it as you slowly exhale. It's as simple as that.

Be forewarned, your mind will intrude upon this exercise by imposing its own stream of thoughts in rapid succession. It might seem difficult to break this cycle, but all it involves is the practice of gently but firmly steering your mind back to the focus of the breath.

This practice will help you restore your sleep cycle and experience a fresh new outlook on life. It will also help you regain your own sense of power oversleep and your life as you realize there is a non-chemical cure for insomnia that actually works.

(4) The Quick Fix Meditation

When in a stressful situation, such as dealing with a boss, colleague, client or personal relationship, one is often unconsciously resisting confrontation in mind and body. This resistance leads to the contraction of the muscles of the body. In order to break this habit of resistance/contraction, one may use the "quick fix meditation", and the results can be astounding.

Become conscious of your posture and thoughts creating, any tension in your body. You'll be surprised at how quickly this becomes apparent.

Consciously loosen in mind and body as you become aware of your breath.

Slow down this breath as you feel it is going in and slowly coming out again. Feel the resistance melt away as you exhale.

This can be achieved in one conscious breath if necessary but understand that the longer you continue, the more the resistance continues melting and eventually disappears. The contracting muscles throughout the body loosen as relaxation replaces tension.

The mind and body fall into sync after this exercise, resulting in the ability to think clearly, make better decisions and see all sides of a conversation rather than the closed down mind of a resistant individual. The result is calmer decisions, constructive thinking, and a cool head: less adrenaline release, fewer anxiety reactions.

The benefits of meditation, even in small increments, are huge. From boosting your immune system to lowering blood pressure and most of all, changing the chemistry of the brain, the rewards are immeasurable. There is a true science behind meditation. It will change brain activity and result in a calmer, less reactive way of thinking. This translates to peace of mind, lower stress triggers and in one word, happiness.

You do not have to make a long term commitment to the art of meditation, but I guarantee you will notice the benefits in short order. You will experience more energy, a true sense of control over all aspects of your life, and a consciously happier sense of self. Relationships will improve calm, peace and relaxed thinking replace stress and tension. One is able to cope in a much more efficient manner with a great less deal effort.

The benefits of this new approach to meditation continue to make it worthwhile in more ways than you can imagine. It is certainly worth a few minutes out of your busy schedule to allow time for an experience leading to a healthier way of thinking and living. Best of all, it is simple, effective and free.

WAYS TO INCREASE FITNESS FOR YOUR BRAIN

Fitness of the brain is as important as the fitness of the body. Various kinds of physical exercises can be done to ensure the fitness of the body. Some important ones among them include strength training, aerobics, stretching, etc. Along with physical exercises; there are exercises that work towards fitness for your brain too. With these exercises, the cognitive abilities of the brain are sharpened and brain functionalities are enhanced as well. Mentioned below are some natural ways by which brainpower and functionalities can be improved:

• Aromatherapy - All of us have heard about aromatherapy. But did you know that aromatherapy could play a pivotal role in enhancing your brain power and brain functionalities? There are numerous essential oils used in aromatherapy, which help in sharpening the brain. For instance, basil or peppermint oil helps in reducing mental fatigue and increases concentration. On the other hand, rosemary oil helps in providing mental alertness and clarity.

• Meditation - Mindful meditation is an excellent way of keeping the mind relaxed and stress-free. Just 30 minutes of meditation on a regular basis can bring in excellent results for the mental and physical well being of individuals. Grey-matter density in the hippocampus increases considerably with meditation. Other attributes, like learning and memory, introspection, compassion, self-awareness, etc., are also bettered with meditation. Along with reducing and controlling stress levels successfully, memory and brain fitness is improved greatly. Neurodegenerative diseases like Alzheimer's, Parkinson's, etc., along with cognitive decline can be managed well with meditation.

• Mind games - You might not know that the human brain is a muscle. And to keep it in good shape and functioning, you need to make the brain exercise as much as possible. Whether it is for memory fitness or increasing cognitive abilities, mind games are simply great tools. Sudoku, scrabble, crosswords, etc., are excellent mind-games, which can sharpen the brain in an excellent manner. These games help in increasing attention, analytical skills, processing speed, positive intellectual and engagement. People who play these games show better memory and problem-solving abilities as they age.

• Sharpening the memory - Memory loss is not solely an age-related problem. Many young people complain of memory loss, and yet they do not take action to improve the same. Using mnemonic devices is an excellent way of keeping things in mind. If you cannot remember things naturally, try remembering them through easier formats like via a concept, in point form, as a list or in words that are familiar to the memory. For memory fitness, each person has their own style of trying things. You can do the one you feel best can help in memory retention.

• De-stressing is very important - If you want to boost your memory and your brain functions naturally, there is no better way than de-stressing. Stress is one of the leading causes of brain cell destruction and memory loss. The brain is functioning continuously by gathering information and data. If it is not allowed to rest and relax, it will not be able to take in new information, let alone to retain the same. Getting proper sleep is very important for de-stressing. Apart from this, there are other ways of shedding off stress too. Choose the ones that seem most suitable for you.

• Eating well is vital - The brain is an organ, which always remains hungry for energy. For optimizing brainpower, it is important that you eat properly and provide the right kind of nutrition to the mind and the body at the same time. Also, drink an abundant amount of water as dehydration can be a potent cause for confusion and memory loss. Eating a healthy and balanced diet will provide the body with all the required nutrients and keep it healthy and happy. Include items in the diet like fish, which is a rich source of

DHA and omega-3 fatty acids. These components help in encouraging the growth of neurons and improve brainpower significantly.

Little changes and modifications in lifestyle can better brainpower and functionalities. Try including them in your life and positive changes are sure to come.

AEROBIC EXERCISES FOR THE BRAIN

Over the past 30 years, some of us have spent hours and hours doing aerobic exercises to maintain our body fitness and keep us looking good. We have attended dance studios, step classes, hi and low impact classes, some of us have even attempted martial arts and water aerobics! In a nutshell, we have put a great deal of time and effort to keep time and nature at bay.

We've accepted it's important to maintain the outward appearance and keep our bodies trim. But what about your mind and brain?

The question is; have you spent the same amount of time on mental aerobics? Have you put in the same amount of effort to keep your mind and brain fit?

Our minds and brains need help too. Just like our bodies, without the right type of exercise they deteriorate, become lethargic, unhealthy and resemble the behavior of a couch potato.

But all is not lost.

Dr. Sara Lazar, a research scientist at the Massachusetts General Hospital in Boston, has discovered a way in which we can keep our brains healthy. Something you can do every day to stop ageing process of your brain. In her research, she used MRI (Magnetic Resonance Imaging) to compare the brain structure of 30 people who lived in and around Boston in the US. She examined 15 people who meditated regularly and 15 people who had never meditated.

She found that meditation:

"increases the thickness of the cortex in areas involved in
attention and sensory processing, such as the pre-frontal cortex
and the right anterior insula".

Now, what does that mean to you and me?

The pre-frontal cortex is the part of the brain that is associated with decision making, planning and memory and naturally thins as we get older, thus reducing our ability to think clearly and make rational decisions.

This research shows that you don't have to be a professional mediator and practice meditation all day to stem the aging process. Anybody can do it.

When you meditate, you are doing a type of aerobics that benefits the brain. Through daily meditation, you are slowing the aging process. You are having an effect on the deterioration of your brain tissue.

The good news is that you don't have to have been meditating for 30 years to gain this benefit. As Dr. Sara Lazar stated in an interview with CNN,

"what we saw is -- the thickness was correlated with the

amount of practice they had. So even people with a just few

years of practice had bigger cortex".

In other words; it's never too late to start.

The secret is to find a meditation practice that suits you. One you enjoy doing. If you had tried meditation before and didn't feel comfortable with that practice, don't give up, try something else. It's the same as physical aerobic exercises; success comes from choosing the method you feel most comfortable with. The more you enjoy it, the more time you will put in and the better the results.

The next step is yours. If you want to stem the aging process of the brain, give yourself time each day to meditate.

EXERCISE EFFECTS ON THE BRAIN AND HOW TO EXERCISE THE BRAIN

The benefits of physical exercise are stupendous when considering brain building and optimal thinking techniques today. A simple solution to optimizing your brain may lie in a disciplined and smart approach to adding physical exercise that will not only make your whole body healthier but improve and maintain cognitive abilities.

Exercise Effects on the Brain

Blood flow is increased to every organ in your body during physical exercise. Dr. Daniel Amen of the Amen Clinics (1) notes how physical exercise will, of course, make the whole body healthier but also actually stimulate neurogenesis and the ability of the body to create new neurons. Even though exercise can relax one from a day's stressful activities, at the same time exercising also can elicit cortical alertness. Good aerobic exercise can even spur your nervous system into a state of arousal.

Now exercise effects on the brain from physical and aerobic activity can be of course a benefit as it could put you in a state ideal for mental activity, but a word of caution here as you certainly wouldn't want to reach this state shortly before some needed deep sleep. It is advised to exercise at least several hours before bedtime, no closer. You want to avoid exercise before bedtime but if you have to exercise before sleep, then reading a book before retiring maybe the correct step but don't choose an excitable book like a murder mystery if you want to sleep soundly after exercise. Many recommend a guided relaxation meditation as an option too.

The Exercise that helps brain activity has been defined as such to keep blood flowing to organs. Covert Bailey (3) has described this aerobic exercise to be at a "comfortable pace" or when your pulse is 220 minus your age and then you take the result and multiply by 0.65 or 0.80 if you are an athlete. Of course, this is only a guide for healthy individuals and people with any health issues would want to consult with their physician as needed. Some general guidelines he noted can be suggested here; the exercise should last at this pace at least 12 minutes while exercising should include the lower body. Note that he recommended the exercise time to be nonstop.

Exercising can be most beneficial at certain times of your day. Before a time when mental alertness is desired and also when the most stressful time of your day is over can both be optimum times to exercise. Get aerobic exercise from brisk walking or even a fitness class for thirty to forty-five minutes a day, five days a week. Most people switch routines for these days, all good.

It is noted that exercise is most beneficial for your brain processing when it is a lifelong activity and you are preserving mental function. Sure, you can start walking regularly at any age, even going to the gym, joining a water aerobics class even after retiring and still get benefits. However, start as early as you can. If you spend a sedentary lifetime, then starting, exercise will not be as effective.

HOW BRAINWAVE ENTRAINMENT CAN AFFECT THE BRAIN

Brainwave entrainment is a scientifically proven neurological tool that induces the brain to mimic a deliberately patterned audio and/or visual stimulus, with the intention of producing a specific state of mind or consciousness. Entrainment, when directed, changes the sculpting of the brain's gray matter, removing old wiring and replacing it with new.

Repeated use of a brainwave entrainment session can cause brain plasticity.

Brain plasticity or neuroplasticity refers to the ability for the brain to make changes in its neural networks, which are due to changes in behavior, environment and neural processes.

Neuroplasticity research indicates that regular entrainment can enhance brain function and structure, and even influence working memory, sense of self, empathy, stress, your level of contentment, and overall quality of life.

Brainwave entrainment, when entraining the brain at a meditative level, ensures physical relaxation and cognitive and psychological benefits, that last long after the session has ended.

The healing of the mind goes beyond the first physical representation of relaxation.

The brain can change and grow and is not static.

Entrainment

In the consciousness state of mindfulness, it reduces the fear center of the brain, rewiring the brain to be steadier and not so reactive, empowering you.

Relieves depression, which dulls your senses, deactivating that area of the brain, while activating a different area of the brain that makes you more aware of your senses.

Grows areas of the brain connected with empathy and compassion.

Fosters the feelings of empathy, giving you great insight, and connection to all-that-is.

Releases serotonin, a happy mood regulator that helps with sleep, calming anxiety, and relieving tension, and controlling obsessions and compulsions.

Reduces the production of cortisol, a stress hormone that can de-activate your immune system and actually encourage cancer and heart disease to progress.

Releases dopamine, providing alertness and energy.

Releases endorphins, the brain's natural painkillers that they are three times stronger than morphine.

Releases oxytocin, which acts as a natural opiate, helping you form emotional and physical connections. It can facilitate orgasm and stimulating sexual experience.

Enables the brain to grow and develop new neural pathways and re-map the connections between these pathways, improving your abilities or changing your thought processes, perceptions and mental/emotional reactions.

Reprograms the mind.

Promotes whole-brain functioning. Both hemispheres are in communication with each other because of new neural pathways developed during entrainment.

Brainwave entrainment affects the brain, permanently forging new neural networks in your gray matter, changing how you experience life. The kicker is that you can choose what goes into these neural networks.

You can choose how you experience your life.

Conclusion

Sometimes it can be hard to distinguish between destructive thoughts, overthinking and anxiety. People have likened these issues to the 'chicken and the egg' situation in that it is difficult to determine what came first; does one have anxiety because they started to overthink things or did they start to overthink things because they suffered with anxiety?

Many people suffer with overthinking on a daily basis without realizing that they are doing it, many people will make hundreds of 'to do' lists telling themselves that they are organized and being prepared. There is nothing wrong with this yet if you are the type to make lists for everything, ask yourself "are you following them?" Are you crossing things off your list and achieving them or are you simply making a list, which you then worry about doing and shortly afterwards make another list without every actually completing anything?

Overthinking can be debilitating, once it starts to hold you back and prevents you from doing the things you want to do then it becomes a problem. However, once you realize you have an issue then you can do something about it.

Our brains are amazing yet being trapped inside our own can horrendous, our own personal hell. Nobody is more negative on ourselves than we are. Start using your overthinking in a positive way; instead of creating problems, try solving them. You can do this by making your to do list but also adding ways to do each item. For example, instead of just writing 'tidy the house' break it into bite size pieces such as 'clean the bath', 'sort out old clothes for the charity' and so on. If it is a work related problem such as meeting a deadline then break it into small chunks, for example, if you are writing a report, put a date to complete each section such as on Monday I'm going to write the introduction, on Tuesday I'm going to gather statistics, and so on.

Another great tool is self-reflection. Many people mix this up with overthinking but self-reflection is healthy when it involves learning about yourself and takes into account both your strengths as well as your weaknesses. Self-reflection allows you to look at a situation in a different way in order to see things from another perspective and used correctly is a great learning tool. Overthinking on the other hand doesn't help you gain new insight or perspective because you are too busy dwelling on the negatives and often worrying about things out of your control.

If you are prone to overthinking then sometimes you just need to halt the mental chatter by switching your thoughts to something else. Mental strength exercises are good for this and there are many resources out there to instruct you in how to do this.

Switching tasks and carrying out a physical activity can be a great way to clear our minds. Some people find relaxing physical activity such as Yoga can empty their thoughts whilst others like something more strenuous like running. Sometimes even just getting up for a short walk can help so if you are stuck in a cycle of negativity and destructive thoughts try getting up and moving about.

The ideas in this book should hopefully have given you something else to focus on but there isn't a 'one size fits all' solution. What works for some doesn't work for everyone and sometimes what works for you one day doesn't work on another day. It really is about trial and error and sticking with it over time.

If you find your overthinking and anxiety is getting the better of you then turn to somebody. We can't always go it alone no matter how independent we want to be. If you have a friend or family member you feel comfortable with then go to them or if you would feel better speaking to somebody completely impartial then you may prefer to see a doctor or a mental health specialist who can help. Whatever you choose, remember there is no shame asking for help and nobody is judging you except you.

www.ingramcontent.com/pod-product-compliance
Lightning Source LLC
Chambersburg PA
CBHW062131020426
42335CB00013B/1179